Study Guide
to accompany

Fundamentals of
The Human Mosaic

Michael Andrew Kukral, Ph.D.
Associate Professor of Geography
Rose-Hulman Institute of Technology

W.H. Freeman and Company
New York

© 2011 W.H. Freeman and Company

ISBN-13: 978-14292-7455-5
ISBN-10: 1-4292-7455-7

Printed in the United States of America

First Printing

W.H. Freeman & Company
41 Madison Avenue
New York, NY 10010
Houndmills, Basingstoke
RG21 6XS England

www.whfreeman.com/geography

CONTENTS

ACKNOWLEDGMENTS

Learning, teaching, experience, and education have always been very important in my family. This brief work is dedicated to the great teachers in my life: my parents. To the memory of my late father, Clarence Ferdinand Kukral, an upholsterer in Cleveland for 62 years; and to the memory of my mother, Ada Mae Kukral, a wonderful person from a farm in Bath, Ohio, who loved art, gardening, and people.

ABOUT THE AUTHOR

Dr. Michael Andrew Kukral is Associate Professor of Geography at Rose-Hulman Institute of Technology. He received his Ph.D. from the University of Kentucky and has been distinguished for teaching excellence at Ohio University, the University of Kentucky, and at Rose-Hulman Institute of Technology.

Dr. Kukral was a Fulbright Scholar in the Czech capital of Prague during the "Velvet Revolution" and is the author of the book *Prague 1989: Theater of Revolution, A Study in Humanistic Political Geography,* published by Columbia University Press. He has traveled extensively in continental Europe and has taught field study courses and led student travel programs there. Since 1999, Professor Kukral has been director of the geography program at Rose-Hulman Institute of Technology, one of our nation's top engineering, math, and science colleges.

A native of the Cuyahoga Valley of Ohio and a member of the Revere High School Hall of Fame, Mike Kukral is also a noted authority on the history, restoration, and music of the player piano and since 2003 has served as editor of the Bulletin of the Automatic Musical Instruments Collectors' Association (see www.amica.org). He enjoys spending time in coastal Oregon and likes hiking, camping, cooking, music, backpacking, and spending time with his family and gray cats, Kitty, Oliver, and Cairo.

PREFACE

A Note to My Colleagues

There is no standard format for writing study guides. After perusing about a dozen guides and talking with many of my former and current students at the University of Kentucky, Ohio Wesleyan University, Rose-Hulman Institute of Technology, and Ohio University, I recognized two common problems that I seek to alleviate in this work.

First, many study guides replicate and summarize the textbook and are simply too lengthy (and thus an expensive addition to the textbook). Several students told me that when study guides are overly thorough, they find little reason to use or purchase the textbook. This can lead to serious problems in student comprehension of text and course material, especially given the highly visual nature of most texts in geography.

Second, some study guides designed for college introductory courses contain too many outside projects and assignments. The problem with this extraneous material is that students rarely use it. Most students in an introductory geography course are not geography majors (unfortunately) and already have enough trouble completing the assignments from their instructor. I have never met a student who has completed a study guide project on his or her own initiative.

My intention with this guide is to provide a simple and hopefully useful method for students to better understand the maps, concepts, and vocabulary of the textbook. Most students I questioned concluded that the most useful portions of any study guide were sections on key terms and the practice tests. I have expanded both of these sections from the length found in the average study guide. In addition, a new and innovative section on reading and interpreting selected maps from the textbook is included.

In summary, the value of any study guide is measured by its ability to help students better understand the textbook. Study guides cannot be written to cover other course material because non-text material is always included at the instructor's discretion. In the field of geography, as we all know, this material can be extremely diverse.

I welcome your comments, ideas, and especially criticisms of this study guide for the purpose of improving subsequent editions. Please contact me directly at Kukral@Rose-Hulman.edu.

To the Student: How to Use This Guide

There is no standard method of studying that works for everyone, but there are many methods of studying that work for many people. Some students study best either while listening to music, at the library, sitting outside, with a study partner, or in the privacy of their room. Despite the location you select, your study methods and techniques determine your ability to succeed in college. Using this study guide presents one such method of textbook comprehension and retention of text information.

Follow this plan of attack for using the *Study Guide to Accompany Fundamentals of The Human Mosaic:*

1. **Preview** *Fundamentals of The Human Mosaic* before beginning your first assignment. This basically involves looking through the book, reading some brief sections that catch your attention, and becoming familiar with the organization of the book. You should note the sections of the book such as contents, preface, index, and most importantly, the marginal glossary (which includes all the book's key terms and their definitions). Be sure to use the glossary frequently! Also be sure to note the five themes used throughout the text: culture region, cultural diffusion, cultural ecology, cultural interaction, and cultural landscape.

2. When you are given a reading assignment from *Fundamentals of The Human Mosaic,* follow this logical pattern:

   a. Preview the chapter to get an idea what it is about.

   b. Attentively read the chapter, perhaps in sections.

   c. Take notes, ask yourself questions, and highlight key statements while reading or rereading the chapter. (Do not highlight everything that seems important or it all becomes ugly and meaningless!)

   d. Do NOT gloss over maps, diagrams, and photographs. These are very important to geographers and they really summarize an enormous amount of information if you interpret them correctly, thoughtfully, and thoroughly.

   e. Now you may begin using the Study Guide to enhance your textbook reading. Complete all initial sections of the Study Guide chapter *before* taking the Practice Tests.

   f. Review the textbook chapter. Now you are ready to determine your progress by taking the Practice Tests. Do NOT look for the answers in the textbook while you are taking the tests. This will not help you (it is like cheating at solitaire).

   g. Check your Practice Test answers with the answer key in the back of the Study Guide. Review your answer selections, especially the ones you missed, and learn from your mistakes. Rewrite your incorrect answers. Review the textbook chapter once more, rewrite your notes, get some sleep, and never miss class.

CHAPTER 1

CULTURAL GEOGRAPHY: AN INTRODUCTION
Extended Chapter Outline (including key terms)

I. Definition and Historic Development of Geography
   A. The growth and development of geography

II. What is Cultural Geography?
   A. Learned collective behavior
   B. Spatial variation and spatial pattern
   C. Physical environments
   D. The example of wheat cultivation

III. Culture Region
   A. Definition of culture region
   B. Formal culture regions: border zones and core-periphery patterns
   C. Functional culture regions: nodes
   D. Vernacular culture regions: perceived regions

IV. Cultural Diffusion
   A. Diffusion: Spatial spread of learned ideas, innovations, attitudes
   B. Independent invention
   C. Expansion diffusion and relocation diffusion: stimulus, hierarchical, and contagious diffusion
   D. Time-distance decay: absorbing and permeable barriers
   E. Migration
   F. Globalization: uneven development

V. Cultural Ecology
   A. Ecosystem
   B. Cultural adaptation
   C. Environmental determinism
   D. Possibilism
   E. Environmental perception: natural hazards
   F. Humans as modifiers of the Earth

VI. Cultural Interaction
   A. Social science: space, models
   B. Humanistic: place, topophilia

VII.   Cultural Landscape
  A. Symbolic landscapes
  B. Three principal aspects of cultural landscape
    1. Settlement forms: nucleation, dispersal
    2. Land-division patterns
    3. Architectural styles

LEARNING OBJECTIVES

After reading this chapter *and* studying the maps and illustrations, you should be able to:

1. Briefly trace the historical development of geography.

2. Define "geography" and how geographers approach the study of Earth and its people.

3. Grasp the meaning of cultural geography and understand its basic topics, themes, and areas of study.

4. Describe, outline, compare, and give examples from the five major themes of cultural geography: culture region, cultural diffusion, cultural ecology, cultural interaction, and cultural landscape.

5. Begin to use the Internet and maps as essential tools of your education and understanding of the world.

SELECTED MAP READING AND INTERPRETATION

This section of the Study Guide is intended to heighten your map reading and interpretation skills. It will also help you apply the text readings to visual and spatial display of concepts, themes, and examples in human and cultural geography.

A world atlas (in print or online) will be very useful in completing this section of the Study Guide and will enhance your comprehension of the maps in the textbook. Ask your instructor to recommend an appropriate web site or atlas to purchase (or visit the map collection at your library). A world atlas is essential for your personal reference library, not only during this course, but throughout your college career.

After reading the text and then studying the accompanying map and its captions, answer the following questions.

FIGURE 1.2. Areas of wheat production in the world today

1. What is the specific single trait on which this map is based?

   _____

   _____

2. What is the scale of this map?

   a. Local   b. Regional   c. Global   d. Continental

3. Are there any spatial patterns of wheat production evident at this scale? For example, is wheat cultivation stronger in the Tropics (between the Tropic of Cancer and the Tropic of Capricorn) or in the temperate latitudes (between the latitudes of 23½ degrees and 66½ degrees North or South)?

   _____

   _____

   _____

4. According to the map, where are the areas of significant wheat production in Africa, North America, and Russia?

   _____

   _____

   _____

FIGURE 1.4. Formal regions of Europe based on only two traits: language and religion

1. What are the three major branches of Christianity portrayed on this map?

   _____, _____, _____

2. What are the three major language families on this map?

   _____, _____, _____

3. Explain what is shown and indicated by the yellow areas on this map.

_____

_____

_____

4. State the two traits for the following countries.

Spain: _____ and _____
Poland: _____ and _____
Norway: _____ and _____
Austria: _____ and _____

5. What theme or themes in human geography does this map illustrate?

_____

_____

_____

FIGURE 1.6. East vs. west and north vs. south in Germany

1. Which two lines of cultural-historical demarcation roughly correspond to the former Iron Curtain? _____ and _____

2. Catholic majorities are located in Austria, _____, and _____.

3. What theme or themes in human geography does this map illustrate?

_____

_____

_____

FIGURE 1.9 Diffusion of HIV/AIDS in Ohio, 1982–1990

1. Explain the hierarchical diffusion of AIDS in Ohio as shown on this map.

_____

_____

_____

2. Are the effects of contagious diffusion evident here? Describe and explain.

_____

_____

_____

3. What factors may explain the lower number of AIDS cases in southeastern Ohio?

_____

_____

_____

4. Does this map tell us that AIDS is an urban-based disease? Why or why not?

_____

_____

_____

FIGURE 1.10. World map of the HDI, 2007

1. Find the countries of Afghanistan and Iraq. Why do you think they stand out on this map when compared to their neighbors such as Iran?

_____

_____

_____

2. What surprises you about this map and why? Give an example from each continent.

_____

_____

_____

3. Can you find any patterns in Africa that may reflect various environments or biomes such as tropical rainforest or desert?

_____

_____

_____

FIGURE 1.12. Chongqing (Chungking) and San Francisco

1. Explain the contrasting appearance of street patterns on both maps.

_____

_____

_____

2. Are either of these street patterns a good case for environmental determinism? Why or why not?

_____

_____

_____

3. Which street system is more practical? Explain.

_____

_____

_____

MATCHING EXERCISES

Match each key term from the text to its definition. Answers are found at the end of this Study Guide.

Set 1

____ 1. absorbing barrier

a. The exterior and interior designs and layouts of the cultural/physical landscape.

____ 2. adaptive strategy

b. A barrier that completely halts diffusion of innovations and blocks the spread of cultural elements.

____ 3. architectural style

c. A concept based on the tendency of both formal and functional culture regions to consist of a core or node, in which defining traits are purest or functions are headquartered, and a periphery that is tributary and displays fewer of the defining traits.

____ 4. border zones

d. A type of expansion diffusion in which cultural innovation spreads by person-to-person contact, moving wavelike through an area and population without regard to social status.

____ 5. contagious diffusion

e. The unique way in which each culture uses its particular physical environment; those aspects of culture that serve to provide the necessities of life—food, clothing, shelter, and defense.

____ 6. core-periphery

f. The areas where different regions meet and sometimes overlap.

Set 2

____ 7. cultural adaptation

a. The adaptation of humans and cultures to the challenges posed by the physical environment.

____ 8. cultural diffusion

b. Broadly defined, the study of the relationships between the physical environment and culture; narrowly (and more commonly) defined, the study of culture as an adaptive system that facilitates human adaptation to nature and environmental change.

____ 9. cultural ecology

c. The study of spatial variations among cultural groups and the spatial functioning of society.

____ 10. cultural geography

d. The relationship of various elements within a culture.

____ 11. cultural interaction

e. The spread of elements of culture from the point of origin over an area.

____ 12. cultural landscape

f. The artificial landscape; the visible human imprint on the land.

7

Set 3

_____ 13. culture

a. A geographical unit based on characteristics and functions of culture.

_____ 14. culture region

b. A type of settlement form in which people live relatively distant from each other.

_____ 15. dispersed

c. A total way of life held in common by a group of people, including such learned features as speech, ideology, behavior, livelihood, technology, and government; or the local, customary way of doing things—a way of life; an ever-changing process in which a group is actively engaged; a dynamic mix of symbols, beliefs, speech, and practices.

_____ 16. ecosystem

d. The belief that culture depends more on what people perceive the environment to be than on the actual character of the environment; perception, in turn, is colored by the teachings of culture.

_____ 17. environmental determinism

e. A territorially bounded system consisting of interacting organic and inorganic components.

_____ 18. environmental perception

f. The belief that cultures are directly or indirectly shaped by the physical environment.

Set 4

_____ 19. expansion diffusion

a. A type of expansion diffusion in which innovations spread from one important person to another or from one urban center to another, temporarily bypassing other persons or rural areas.

_____ 20. formal culture region

b. The spread of innovations within an area in a snowballing process, so that the total number of knowers or users becomes greater and the area of occurrence grows.

_____ 21. functional culture region

c. The binding together of all the lands and peoples of the world into an integrated system driven by capitalistic free markets, in which cultural diffusion is rapid, independent states are weakened, and cultural homogenization is encouraged.

_____ 22. geography

d. A cultural region inhabited by people who have one or more cultural traits in common.

_____ 23. globalization

e. The study of spatial patterns and of differences and similarities from one place to another in environment and culture.

_____ 24. hierarchical diffusion

f. A cultural area that functions as a unit politically, socially, or economically.

Set 5

_____ 25. independent invention

a. The large-scale movements of people between different regions of the world.

_____ 26. land-division pattern

b. A term that refers to the spatial patterns of different land uses.

_____ 27. migrations

c. An abstraction, an imaginary situation, proposed by geographers to simulate laboratory conditions so that they may isolate certain causal forces for detailed study.

_____ 28. model

d. A cultural innovation that is developed in two or more locations by individuals or groups working independently.

_____ 29. natural hazard

e. An inherent danger present in a given habitat, such as flooding, hurricanes, volcanic eruptions, or earthquakes; often perceived differently by different peoples.

_____ 30. neighborhood effect

f. Microscale diffusion in which acceptance of an innovation is most rapid in small clusters around an initial adopter.

Set 6

_____ 31. node

a. A school of thought based on the belief that humans, rather than the physical environment, are the primary active force; that any environment offers a number of different possible ways for a culture to develop; and that the choices among these possibilities are guided by cultural heritage.

_____ 32. nucleation

b. A term used to connote the subjective, idiographic, humanistic, culturally oriented type of geography that seeks to understand the unique character of individual regions and places, rejecting the principles of science as flawed and unknowingly biased.

_____ 33. permeable barrier

c. A central point in a functional culture region where functions are coordinated and directed.

_____ 34. physical environment

d. All aspects of the natural physical surroundings, such as climate, terrain, soils, vegetation, and wildlife.

_____ 35. place

e. A barrier that permits some aspects of an innovation to diffuse through it but weakens and retards continued spread; an innovation can be modified in passing through a permeable barrier.

_____ 36. possibilism

f. A relatively dense settlement form.

Set 7

_____ 37. relocation diffusion

a. The spatial arrangement of buildings, roads, towns, and other features that people construct while inhabiting an area.

_____ 38. settlement forms

b. Landscapes that express the values, beliefs, and meanings of a particular culture.

_____ 39. space

c. The decrease in acceptance of a cultural innovation with increasing time and distance from its origin.

_____ 40. stimulus diffusion

d. The spread of an innovation or other element of culture that occurs with the bodily relocation (migration) of the individual or group responsible for the innovation.

_____ 41. symbolic landscapes

e. A type of expansion diffusion in which a specific trait fails to spread but the underlying idea or concept is accepted.

_____ 42. time-distance decay

f. A term used to connote the objective, quantitative, theoretical, model-based, economics-oriented type of geography that seeks to understand spatial systems and networks through application of the principles of social science.

Set 8

_____ 43. topophilia

a. The tendency for industry to develop in a core-periphery pattern, enriching the industrialized countries of the core and impoverishing the less industrialized periphery. This term is also used to describe urban patterns in which suburban areas are enriched while the inner city is impoverished.

_____ 44. uneven development

b. Love of place; used to describe people who exhibit a strong sense of place.

_____ 45. vernacular cultural region

c. A cultural region perceived to exist by its inhabitants; based in the collective spatial perception of the population at large; bearing a generally accepted name or nickname (such as "Dixie").

REVIEW: Self-evaluation Tests

PART ONE: Multiple-choice

Circle the best answer for each question. When you are finished, read each question again with your selected answer. After you are satisfied with your practice test, use the Answer Key in the back of the Study Guide to check your responses.

1. Climate, vegetation, terrain, wildlife, and soil and water patterns are all basic components of:
   a. culture.
   b. human geography.
   c. physical environments.
   d. cultural landscape.
   e. absorbing barriers.

2. The word "geography" is a Greek word meaning literally:
   a. to study the Earth.
   b. to describe the Earth.
   c. to study various countries.
   d. to write about the natural environment.
   e. to analyze cultures of the world

3. The authors of your textbook define culture as:
   a. spatial variation of humans.
   b. inherited traits of humans.
   c. traditional lifestyles.
   d. learned human behavior.
   e. human perception and actions.

4. Human geography is the study of the:
   a. spatial variations among cultural groups.
   b. analysis of the physical environment.
   c. relationships between people and places.
   d. built and natural landscapes.
   e. various behavioral traits of humans.

5. A culture region is a geographical unit based in:
   a. characteristics and functions of culture.
   b. traditional patterns.
   c. human traits.
   d. complex behavioral patterns.
   e. physical properties.

6. A French-language region is an example of a:
   a. functional culture region.
   b. formal culture region.
   c. vernacular culture region.
   d. multiple-trait area.
   e. none of the above

11

7. Formal culture regions in geography often display a core-periphery pattern.
   a. True
   b. False

8. Cultural homogeneity is the hallmark of a:
   a. functional culture region.
   b. formal culture region.
   c. vernacular culture region.
   d. multiple-trait area
   e. none of the above

9. Yi-Fu Tuan is a geographer associated with the concept and terms *topophilia* and:
   a. spatial modeling.
   b. quantitative geography.
   c. political landscape.
   d. sense of place
   e. transnational migration.

10. Globalization is a process that really took off in the _____ century.
   a. sixteenth
   b. seventeenth
   c. eighteenth
   d. nineteenth
   e. twentieth

11. Uneven development basically refers to:
   a. the HDI only.
   b. the HDI and GDP.
   c. distribution of resources.
   d. location of countries.
   e. cultural ecology.

12. Nodes, or central points where activities are coordinated and directed, are a common characteristic of a:
   a. functional culture region.
   b. formal culture region.
   c. vernacular culture region.
   d. multiple-trait area.
   e. none of the above

13. Clearly defined borders are a common feature of a:
   a. functional region.
   b. formal region.
   c. vernacular culture region.
   d. multiple-trait area.
   e. none of the above

14. Which of the following is NOT an example of a functional culture region?
    a. coal fields of northern Appalachia
    b. newspaper circulation area
    c. Korean-language area
    d. Cleveland metropolitan area
    e. the state of Laos

15. A vernacular culture region is often considered to be a region:
    a. clearly demarcated on a map.
    b. with strong functional and formal features.
    c. perceived to exist by its inhabitants.
    d. with traditional structural traits.
    e. none of the above

16. Most geographical studies of the cultural landscape have focused on three principal aspects:
    land-division patterns, architecture, and _____ .
    a. barn types
    b. settlement forms
    c. ethnicity
    d. food and drink
    e. spatial-temporal patterns of transportation

17. The wavelike spread of ideas primarily involves the concept of:
    a. stimulus diffusion.
    b. hierarchical diffusion.
    c. contagious diffusion.
    d. absorbing barriers.
    e. none of the above

18. The study of the interaction between culture and environment is termed:
    a. cultural ecology.
    b. neighborhood effect.
    c. environmental science.
    d. humanistic geography.
    e. biogeography.

19. Environmental determinism was a common doctrine of belief among geographers during the:
    a. mid-nineteenth century.
    b. 1950s and 1960s.
    c. late eighteenth century.
    d. early twentieth century.
    e. 1970s.

20. The belief that cultural heritage is at least as important as the physical environment in affecting human behavior is usually associated with:
    a. environmental determinism.
    b. possibilism.
    c. two-trait regions.
    d. single-trait regions.
    e. material landscape.

21. Model building, theory, and space are terms and devices usually associated with the_____ approach in cultural geography.
    a. humanistic
    b. humans as modifiers of the Earth
    c. cultural ecological
    d. landscape interpretation
    e. social science

22. Place, topophilia, sense of place, and subjectivity are terms and ideas usually associated with the _____ approach in cultural geography.
    a. humanistic
    b. humans as modifiers of the Earth
    c. cultural ecological
    d. landscape interpretation
    e. social science

23. The Eiffel Tower in Paris is part of the city skyline. This is an example of a(n):
    a. artistic landscape.
    b. architectural landscape.
    c. symbolic landscape.
    d. transnational urban core.
    e. global heritage site.

PART TWO: Short-answer and fill-in-the-blank (probable essay-type questions)

24. The authors of the textbook are: _____.

25. Culture is defined as:

    _____
    _____
    _____

26. Cultural geography is the study of:

    _____
    _____
    _____

27. The five themes in cultural geography are:
    a. _____
    b. _____
    c. _____

d. _____

e. _____

28. Explain the difference between formal culture regions and functional culture regions.

_____
_____
_____
_____

29. Give an example of a core-periphery pattern.

_____
_____
_____

30. What is globalization?

_____
_____
_____
_____

31. Explain why the German-language region is different from the country of Germany in the perspective of cultural geography.

_____
_____
_____

32. How are vernacular culture regions different from formal and functional culture regions?

_____
_____
_____

33. Explain the difference between hierarchical diffusion and stimulus diffusion:

_____
_____
_____

34. What is meant by time-distance decay?

_____
_____
_____

35. Explain the differences among environmental determinism, cultural ecology, and possibilism.

_____
_____
_____
_____

36. What is humanistic geography?

_____

_____

_____

37. Examples of natural hazards are:

_____

_____

_____

38. What role does "perception" play in studies of cultural ecology?

_____

_____

_____

_____

39. Describe the theme of cultural interaction.

_____

_____

_____

_____

40. Explain the difference between the geographic concepts of "space" and "place."

_____

_____

_____

_____

41. List some actual examples of the cultural landscape known to you.

_____

_____

_____

_____

CHAPTER TWO

FOLK AND POPULAR CULTURES

Extended Chapter Outline (including key terms)

I. Many Cultures: Material, Nonmaterial, Folk, and Popular
  A. Material culture
  B. Nonmaterial culture
  C. Folk culture
  D. Popular culture

II. Folk and Popular Culture Regions
  A. Material folk culture regions
  B. Folk food regions
  C. Is popular culture placeless?
  D. Popular food and drink
  E. Popular music
  F. Vernacular culture regions

III. Folk and Popular Culture Diffusion
  A. Diffusion in folk culture: agricultural fairs
  B. Diffusion in popular culture
  C. Advertising
  D. Communications barriers
  E. Diffusion of the rodeo
  F. Blowguns: diffusion or independent invention?

IV. The Ecology of Folk and Popular Culture
  A. Folk medicine and ecology
  B. Nature in popular culture

V. Cultural Interaction in Folk and Popular Cultures
  A. Country and western music
  B. Difference to convergence: convergence hypothesis
  C. Difference revitalized: local consumption cultures, consumer nationalism
  D. Place images

VI. Folk and Popular Cultural Landscapes
  A. Folk architecture
  B. Folk housing in North America
  C. Folk housing in Africa south of the Sahara
  D. Landscapes of popular culture
  E. Leisure landscapes, amenity landscapes
  F. Elitist landscapes

LEARNING OBJECTIVES

After reading this chapter *and* studying the maps and illustrations, you should be able to:

1. Define, identify, and describe folk and popular culture and their respective regions and landscapes.

2. Understand and explain various examples of folk and popular culture diffusion.

3. Describe the relationship between nature and folk and popular cultures.

4. Provide examples and explain how globalization integrates various cultural practices.

5. Discuss how the cultural landscape is shaped and affected by folk and popular cultures.

6. Recognize the role of globalization and folk and popular culture in your own family, region, or heritage.

SELECTED MAP READING AND INTERPRETATION

This section of the Study Guide is intended to heighten your map reading and interpretation skills. It will also help you apply the text readings to visual and spatial display of concepts, themes, and examples in human and cultural geography.

A world atlas (in print or online) will be very useful in completing this section of the Study Guide and will enhance your comprehension of the maps in the textbook. Ask your instructor to recommend an appropriate web site or atlas to purchase (or visit the map collection at your library). A world atlas is essential for your personal reference library, not only during this course, but throughout your college career.

After reading the text and then studying the accompanying map and its captions, answer the following questions.

FIGURE 2.1. *Folk cultural survival regions of the United States and southern Canada*

1. Identify the folk culture of your local region. Can you think of any examples of existing or former evidence of material folk culture?

   _____
   _____
   _____

2. From north to south, what are the folk culture regions of the Rocky Mountains?

   _____
   _____
   _____

3. What are the two locations of Acadian French folk culture? What is another name used for this culture in some locales?

   _____
   _____
   _____

FIGURE 2.8. *Three examples of the 40 lifestyle clusters in U.S. popular culture*

1. How was the data collected for the creation of this map?

   _____
   _____
   _____

2. What are the definitions of "Gray Power," "Old Yankee Rows," and "Norma Rae –Ville"?

   _____
   _____
   _____

3. How do you see this map changing during the next twenty years? Has it changed already?

_____

_____

_____

FIGURE 2.9. Fast-food sales as a share of total restaurant sales, by state

1. What might account for the spatial variation in this aspect of popular culture?

_____

_____

_____

2. Does this pattern bear any similarity to the map of traditional and folk cultures shown in Figure 2.1?

_____

_____

_____

3. What does this suggest about the convergence hypothesis, which holds that regional cultures in America are collapsing into a national or global culture?

_____

_____

_____

FIGURE 2.12. The vernacular of the Middle West or Midwest

1. What might account for the differences between this map and Figure 2.11?

_____

_____

_____

2. Why would some respondents (less than 10 percent) claim to live in the Midwest in states such as Florida, California, and New Hampshire?

_____

_____

_____

3. Which states on this map, such as Ohio, can be considered on the Midwest periphery? Why?

_____

_____

_____

FIGURE 2.16. Former distribution of the blowgun

1. Were the two widely separated areas of blowgun use the result of independent invention or cultural diffusion?

   _____

   _____

   _____

2. Can you think of any reasons for the lack of blowgun use in continental Africa, Australia, or southern South America?

   _____

   _____

   _____

MATCHING EXERCISES

Match each key term from the text to its definition. Answers are found at the end of this Study Guide.

Set 1

_____ 1. amenity landscapes

a. The forceful appropriation of a territory by a distant state, often involving the displacement of indigenous populations to make way for colonial settlers.

_____ 2. colonialism

b. Landscapes that are prized for their natural and cultural aesthetic qualities by the tourism and real estate industries and their customers.

_____ 3. consumer nationalism

c. A hypothesis holding that cultural differences among places are being reduced by improved transportation and communications systems, leading to a homogenization of popular culture.

_____ 4. convergence hypothesis

d. A situation where local consumers favor nationally produced goods over imported goods as part of a nationalist political agenda.

_____ 5. folk

e. Structures built by members of a folk society or culture in a traditional manner and style, without the assistance of professional architects or blueprints, using locally available raw materials.

_____ 6. folk architecture

f. Traditional, rural; the opposite of "popular."

Set 2

_____ 7. folk culture

a. Distinct consumption practices and preferences in food, clothing, music, and so forth formed in specific places and historical moments.

_____ 8. folk geography

b. The wide range of tales, songs, lore, beliefs, superstitions, and customs that passes from generation to generation as part of an oral or written tradition.

_____ 9. leisure landscapes

c. All physical, tangible objects made and used by members of a cultural group, such as clothing, buildings, tools and utensils, instruments, furniture, and artwork; the visible aspect of culture.

_____ 10. local consumption cultures

d. A small, cohesive, stable, isolated, nearly self-sufficient group that is homogeneous in custom and race; characterized by a strong family or clan structure, order maintained through sanctions based in the religion or family, little division of labor other than that between the sexes, frequent and strong interpersonal relationships, and a material culture consisting mainly of handmade goods.

_____ 11. material culture   e. The study of the spatial patterns and ecology of traditional groups; a branch of cultural geography.

_____ 12. nonmaterial culture   f. Landscapes that are planned and designed primarily for entertainment purposes, such as ski and beach resorts.

Set 3

_____ 13. placelessness   a. A dynamic culture based in large, heterogeneous societies permitting considerable individualism, innovation, and change; having a money-based economy, division of labor into professions, secular institutions of control, and weak interpersonal ties; producing and consuming machine-made goods.

_____ 14. popular culture   b. A culture region perceived to exist by its inhabitants; based in the collective spatial perception of the population at large; bearing a generally accepted name or nickname (such as "Dixie").

_____ 15. subculture   c. A group of people with norms, values, and material practices that differentiate them from the dominant culture to which they belong.

_____ 16. vernacular culture region   d. A spatial standardization that diminishes regional variety; may result from the spread of popular culture, which can diminish or destroy the uniqueness of place through cultural standardization on a national or even worldwide scale.

REVIEW: Self-evaluation Tests

PART ONE: Multiple-choice

Circle the best answer for each question. When you are finished, read each question again with your selected answer. After you are satisfied with your practice test, use the Answer Key in the back of the Study Guide to check your responses.

1. The best active example of a folk culture in the United States is the:
   a. Hispanic culture of the Southwest.
   b. Cuban culture in Florida.
   c. Amish culture in Ohio and Pennsylvania.
   d. African-American culture in the Lower South.
   e. family farm of the Midwest.

2. Food, tools, furniture, buildings, and clothing are all considered:
   a. material culture.
   b. folklore.
   c. living history.
   d. folk geography.
   e. none of the above

3. Folk dialects, religions, and worldviews can be regarded as:
   a. traditional lifestyles.
   b. popular culture.
   c. cultural artifacts.
   d. nonmaterial culture.
   e. none of the above

4. Many remnants of folk cultures are found in North America.
   a. True
   b. False

5. Perhaps the most enduring feature of folk culture is:
   a. architecture.
   b. language.
   c. clothing.
   d. occupation.
   e. food.

6. Folk culture spreads by the same processes of diffusion as do other elements and types of culture, but more rapidly.
   a. True
   b. False

7. If one or more nonfunctional features of blowguns occurred in both South America and Indonesia, then it is logical to surmise that the distribution of blowguns:
   a. is based on the theory of independent-invention.
   b. is independent of functionality.

c. is a result of diffusion.

d. occurred after the year 1492.

e. none of the above

8. In southern Africa, this term often refers to a group or compound of buildings.

   a. kraal

   b. ndebele

   c. hausa

   d. transvaal

   e. station

9. Country and western music in the United States has its origins in the folk culture of the:

   a. upper Midwest.

   b. Gulf Coast.

   c. Rocky Mountains.

   d. Great Lakes.

   e. Upland South.

10. A spatial standardization that diminishes cultural variety and demeans the human spirit can result in:

    a. place image.

    b. non-place image.

    c. placelessness.

    d. aspatial values.

    e. popular culture .

11. According to the text, the leading region or places for beer consumption in the United States is (are):

    a. the Lower South.

    b. the upper Midwest.

    c. California and Florida.

    d. the Northeast.

    e. the Southwest.

12. Regions perceived to exist by their inhabitants are termed:

    a. popular regions.

    b. vernacular regions.

    c. folk regions.

    d. perceived regions.

    e. psychological regions.

13. Resentment toward imported goods can be termed:

    a. racist.

    b. consumer nationalism.

    c. post-consumption culture.

    d. anti-globalization.

    e. material xenophobia.

14. Time-distance decay in popular culture diffusion is _____ folk culture.
    a. stronger than
    b. considerably stronger than
    c. weaker than
    d. considerably weaker than
    e. about the same as

15. Popular culture is considered to have a _____ rate of diffusion.
    a. slow
    b. average
    c. rapid
    d. lateral
    e. dynamic

16. The rodeo, as an example of popular culture diffusion, has its origins in:
    a. Spanish settlement areas.
    b. primarily Texas.
    c. Montana and Oklahoma.
    d. southern California.
    e. Both b and c are correct.

17. Of the following European countries, which probably do not participate much in Western popular culture?
    a. Czech Republic, Lithuania, Austria
    b. Switzerland, France, Luxembourg
    c. Norway, Finland, Estonia
    d. Germany, Poland, Belgium
    e. none of the above

18. Popular culture, by definition, does not display regionalization.
    a. True
    b. False

19. The devices of diffusion in popular culture require large amounts of electricity and fossil fuels.
    a. True
    b. False

20. Popular culture makes exceedingly high demands on:
    a. national parks.
    b. wilderness areas.
    c. coastal zones.
    d. national recreation areas.
    e. all of the above

21. Many social scientists assume that the results of causal forces in popular culture would be to homogenize culture. This view is called:
    a. placelessness.
    b. time-distance continuum.

c. clustering.
d. convergence hypothesis.
e. none of the above

22. Photography, literature, television, and film often contribute to the creation of:
    a. peripheral place zones.
    b. tourist illiteracy.
    c. place image.
    d. the modernity hypothesis.
    e. none of the above

23. Which of the following would probably be labeled as a gentleman farm?
    a. sheep ranching for wool production
    b. horticulture of nuts and fruits
    c. fish farming in the Mississippi
    d. thoroughbred horse breeding in Kentucky
    e. organic farming

24. In stage 5 of Jakle and Mattson's model of commercial strip evolution:
    a. the residential function disappears.
    b. the commercial function dominates.
    c. gas stations are introduced.
    d. single-family residences dominate.
    e. none of the above

25. The most reflective landscape of consumption in popular culture is the:
    a. commercial strip.
    b. shopping mall.
    c. central business district (CBD).
    d. gentleman farm.
    e. hotel and convention complexes.

26. Stones are often used as the traditional building material of the farmers of:
    a. northern Europe.
    b. Russia.
    c. Canada.
    d. the Mediterranean.
    e. Southeast Asia.

27. The ndebele house ornamentation is a good indicator of traditional:
    a. stone construction
    b. half-timbering
    c. communal housing
    d. cultural identity
    e. unit farmstead

28. An example of an African-American folk dwelling is the:
    a. shotgun house.
    b. New England large.

c. upright and wing.
d. traditional Georgian.
e. saddlebag house.

29. As Yankee folk migrated westward, they developed this type of house:
    a. shotgun house
    b. New England large
    c. upright and wing
    d. traditional Georgian
    e. saddlebag house

PART TWO: Short-answer (probable essay-type questions)

30. Provide some examples of both material and nonmaterial culture.

_____
_____
_____

31. Briefly describe the difference between folk and popular culture.

_____
_____
_____

32. List some of the defining elements of popular culture.

_____
_____
_____

33. Provide an example and define "placelessness."

_____
_____
_____

34. What is the role of popular music in the geography of popular culture?

_____
_____
_____

35. Discuss the regional variation of rodeos in the United States.

_____
_____
_____

36. What is a vernacular culture region and how do they apply to popular culture?

_____
_____
_____

37. Discuss the role of advertising in the process of diffusion.

_____

_____

_____

38. What are some barriers to the diffusion of popular culture?

_____

_____

_____

39. What are some of the environmental influences on popular culture?

_____

_____

_____

40. State some specific examples of popular culture's impact on the environment.

_____

_____

_____

41. Explain the convergence hypothesis. Do you agree with it?

_____

_____

_____

42. What is a place image and how are place images created?

_____

_____

_____

43. Provide some characteristics of an elitist landscape.

_____

_____

_____

44. What is a landscape of consumption?

_____

_____

_____

45. Provide a definition and example of a leisure landscape.

_____

_____

_____

46. What are some examples of popular culture in your home area?

_____

_____

_____

47. Why do you think American pop culture has become an international phenomenon?

_____

_____

_____

48. As North Americans, what features of other countries' popular culture do we absorb?

_____

_____

_____

49. What are some of the traditional folk culture regions of the United States?

_____

_____

_____

50. Discuss some culture elements and provide an example of a folk food region.

_____

_____

_____

51. Use folk songs to demonstrate the process of folk cultural diffusion.

_____

_____

_____

52. Briefly explain the two conflicting ideas or theories concerning the global distribution of the blowgun.

_____

_____

_____

53. What are reasons behind the cultural practice of "gentlemen farms"?

_____

_____

_____

54. What are three major contributions to the folk geography of the United States attributed to the Upland South region?

_____

_____

_____

55. Select an area of the world outside of North America and describe the traditional building materials and their relationship to the natural environment.

_____

_____

_____

CHAPTER THREE

POPULATION GEOGRAPHY
Extended Chapter Outline (including key terms)

I. Demographic Regions
    A. Population distribution and density
        1. Population density
        2. Formal demographic regions
        3. Carrying capacity
    B. Patterns of natality
        1. Birthrates
        2. Fertility rates
        3. Zero population growth
    C. The geography of mortality: death rates
    D. Population explosion?
    E. Demographic transition
    F. Age distributions: population pyramids
    G. Geography of gender
        1. Sex ratio
        2. Gender roles
    H. Standard of living: infant mortality rate

II. Diffusion in Population Geography
    A. Migration
        1. The decision to move
        2. Push-and-pull factors
    B. Disease diffusion: example of HIV/AIDS

III. Population Ecology
    A. Environmental influence
        1. Climatic factors
        2. Coastal locations
    B. Environmental perception and population distribution
    C. Population density and environmental alteration

IV. Cultural Interaction and Population Patterns
    A. Cultural factors
    B. Political and economic factors
    C. Population control programs

V. The Settlement Landscape
    A. Farm villages
        1. Farmsteads and clustered settlements
        2. Environmental determinants
    B. Isolated farmsteads
    C. Historical factors
    D. Gender

LEARNING OBJECTIVES

After reading this chapter *and* studying the maps and illustrations, you should be able to:

1. Understand the terms and concepts used by geographers to study the human population.

2. Give examples of the various factors influencing human migration and population mobility.

3. Distinguish and discuss the differences among population distribution, population density, and population composition.

4. Show the relationship between population and the environment, including factors of human perception and gender.

5. Understand the role of political, economic, and especially cultural phenomena in influencing the human population.

6. Distinguish various settlement patterns and farm village patterns.

7. Continue to improve your ability to read and interpret the cultural landscape.

SELECTED MAP READING AND INTERPRETATION

This section of the Study Guide is intended to heighten your map reading and interpretation skills. It will also help you apply the text readings to visual and spatial display of concepts, themes, and examples in human and cultural geography.

A world atlas (in print or online) will be very useful in completing this section of the Study Guide and will enhance your comprehension of the maps in the textbook. Ask your instructor to recommend an appropriate web site or atlas to purchase (or visit the map collection at your library). A world atlas is essential for your personal reference library, not only during this course, but throughout your college career.

After reading the text and then studying the accompanying map and its captions, answer the following questions.

FIGURE 3.1. *Population density in the world*

1. It is well-known that China has the largest population in the world. The pattern of population distribution in China, however, shows a clear East-West division. Can you think of any environmental or economic factors influencing this pattern in China? Secondly, do you see a similar distribution pattern in the United States, Brazil, and Australia? Provide a few statements to support your answer.

   _____

   _____

   _____

   _____

2. Is it reasonable to state that population density is usually highest in coastal regions? Select a few specific countries or regions to support your answer.

   _____

   _____

   _____

3. What is the pattern of population density in the tropics? Use the continents of Africa, Asia, and South America in your answer.

   _____

   _____

   _____

4. Can you think of any reasons for the band of high population density running across the interior of Central Europe?

   _____

   _____

   _____

FIGURE 3.3. The total fertility rate (TFR) in the world

1. What regions of the world have the highest TFR?

    _____

    _____

2. Can you think of any reasons why some Latin American countries, such as Honduras, have higher TFR than others?

    _____

    _____

    _____

3. Compare the data on this map with the data shown in Figure 3.1. Does this comparison illustrate that the population of China and India must be declining? Why or why not?

    _____

    _____

    _____

FIGURE 3.4. The Geography of HIV/AIDS

1. What is the population density of the countries with the highest rate of HIV/AIDS?

    _____

    _____

    _____

2. Where is HIV/AIDS lowest according to this map? Can you make some suggestions for the low numbers? What role does government have in reporting these numbers?

    _____

    _____

    _____

    _____

3. Can you find a relationship between HIV/AIDS and the economy of a region or country? Any examples?

    _____

    _____

    _____

FIGURE 3.9. Geography of contraception in the modern world

1. Where do the highest percentages occur? Are these rich or poor areas?

    _____

    _____

    _____

2. The white areas on this map are an indication of what?

_____

_____

3. Compare this map with Figure 3.3. What can you interpret from this comparison?

_____

_____

_____

FIGURE 3.10. *The world pattern of youth and old age*

1. Do these maps show a relationship between economy and age? Why or why not? Compare Europe and Africa.

_____

_____

_____

2. What probably accounts for the older populations living in West Virginia, Florida, and Pennsylvania? Explain.

_____

_____

_____

3. Can you think of any cultural or environmental reasons for the patterns on these maps?

_____

_____

_____

MATCHING EXERCISES

Match each key term from the text to its definition. Answers are found at the end of this Study Guide.

Set 1

_____ 1. birthrate

a. The maximum number of people that can be supported in a given area.

_____ 2. carrying capacity

b. The annual number of deaths per 1000 persons in the population.

_____ 3. death rate

c. The annual number of births per 1000 persons in the population.

_____ 4. demographic transition

d. A clustered rural settlement of moderate size, inhabited by people who are engaged in farming.

_____ 5. farmstead

e. The center of farm operations, containing the house, barn, sheds, and livestock pens.

_____ 6. farm village

f. A term used to describe the movement from high birth and death rates to low birth and death rates.

Set 2

_____ 7. formal demographic region

a. The amount of space that individuals feel "belong" to them as they move about their daily business.

_____ 8. gender roles

b. The number of infants per 1000 live births who die before reaching one year of age.

_____ 9. geodemography

c. Population geography; the study of the spatial and ecological aspects of population, including distribution, density per unit of land area, fertility, gender, health, age, mortality, and migration.

_____ 10. infant mortality rate

d. A demographic region based on the single trait of population density.

_____ 11. Malthusian

e. Those who hold the views of Thomas Malthus, who believed that overpopulation is the root cause of poverty, illness, and warfare.

_____ 12. personal space

f. What it means to be a man, and what it means to be a woman, in different cultural and historical contexts.

Set 3

_____ 13. population density

a. The rapid, accelerating increase in world population since about 1650 and especially since 1900.

_____ 14. population explosion

b. A graph used to show the age and sex composition of a population.

_____ 15. population geography

c. A measurement of population per unit area (for example, per square mile).

_____ 16. population pyramid

d. Geodemography; the study of the spatial and ecological aspects of population, including distribution, density per unit of land area, fertility, gender, health, age, mortality, and migration.

_____ 17. pull factors

e. Those fleeing from persecution in their country of nationality. The persecution can be religious, political, racial, or ethnic.

_____ 18. push factors

f. Favorable, attractive conditions that interact to affect migration and other elements of diffusion.

_____ 19. refugees

g. Unfavorable, repelling conditions that interact to affect migration and other elements of diffusion.

Set 4

_____ 20. sex ratio

a. The numerical ratio of males to females in a population.

_____ 21. total fertility rate (TFR)

b. A stabilized population created when an average of only two children per couple survive to adulthood, so that, eventually, the number of deaths equals the number of births.

_____ 22. zero population growth

c. The number of children the average woman will bear during her reproductive lifetime (15–44 years old).

REVIEW: Self-evaluation Tests

PART ONE: Multiple-choice

Circle the best answer for each question. When you are finished, read each question again with your selected answer. After you are satisfied with your practice test, use the Answer Key in the back of the Study Guide to check your responses.

1. The current population of the Earth is about:
   a. 2.9 billion.
   b. 9.9 billion.
   c. 4.5 billion.
   d. 12 billion.
   e. 6.8 billion.

2. Population geographers primarily study the _____ aspects of demography.
   a. physical
   b. physiological
   c. ecological
   d. cultural
   e. distributive

3. The five most populous countries are Brazil, United States, China, India, and:
   a. Russia.
   b. Indonesia.
   c. Nigeria.
   d. Germany.
   e. Pakistan.

4. Less than five percent of the world's population lives in the United States.
   a. True
   b. False

5. "Moderately settled areas" have about _____ persons per square mile.
   a. 500–700
   b. 250–500
   c. 60–250
   d. 2–60
   e. none of the above

6. The density beyond which people cease to be nutritionally self-sufficient is said to be above:
   a. carrying capacity.
   b. physiological nutrition.
   c. zero growth.
   d. biological density.
   e. caloric regression.

7. Birth and death rates are measured in number per:
   a. hundred.
   b. thousand.
   c. hundred-thousand.
   d. million.
   e. square mile.

8. The three main population clusters of the world are eastern Asia, the Indian subcontinent, and:
   a. Europe.
   b. China.
   c. the eastern United States.
   d. West Africa.
   e. East Africa.

9. At present rates, about how many years will it take for the world population to double?
   a. 15
   b. 20
   c. 30
   d. 40
   e. 50

10. The American tropics, North Africa, the Middle East, and Central Asia all have _____ death rates.
    a. very high
    b. high
    c. low
    d. average
    e. very low

11. Rapid population growth among humans began around the year:
    a. 1450.
    b. 1930.
    c. 1890.
    d. 1820.
    e. 1700.

12. Malthus stated that famine and _____ would be constant checks of population growth.
    a. natural disasters
    b. poverty
    c. disease
    d. war
    e. accidents

13. In preindustrial societies, birth and death rates are both normally:
    a. high.
    b. low.
    c. moderate.
    d. very low.
    e. none of the above

14. Recently settled areas typically have more males than females.
    a. True
    b. False

15. Living in a farm village places the family on their agricultural land.
    a. True
    b. False

16. The most common type of migration is:
    a. forced.
    b. push-and-pull.
    c. international.
    d. war refugee.
    e. voluntary.

17. The largest migration in history took place in the _____ century, when more than 50 million people left Europe.
    a. twentieth
    b. nineteenth
    c. eighteenth
    d. seventeenth
    e. sixteenth

18. Areas of extremely high heat or cold are considered to be _____ climates from the perspective of humans.
    a. "golden mean"
    b. wonderful
    c. defective
    d. marginal
    e. uninhabitable

19. Americans account for about _____ percent of the world's resources consumed each year.
    a. 5
    b. 10
    c. 15
    d. 20
    e. 40

20. A "cenote" is a:
   a. village public hall.
   b. public cooking area.
   c. skate wheel.
   d. sinkhole.
   e. village elder.

21. Farm villages are common throughout much of the rural American Midwest.
   a. True
   b. False

22. The "street village" is particularly common to:
   a. China.
   b. Russia.
   c. Latin America.
   d. East Africa.
   e. Southeast Asia.

23. Before the Spanish conquest, most Mayans lived in _____ villages.
   a. highland
   b. coastal
   c. isolated
   d. wet-point
   e. common

PART TWO: Short-answer (probable essay type questions)

24. What do population geographers study *and* what topics and processes are included in these studies?

   _____
   _____
   _____

25. Explain the difference between population distribution and population density.

   _____
   _____
   _____

26. How is the fertility rate measured and what can this statistic indicate in regard to population patterns?

   _____
   _____
   _____

27. What is meant by "population explosion," and how and why did this event come about?

_____

_____

_____

28. What are the contributions of Thomas Malthus to demographic studies? Are his ideas valid today?

_____

_____

_____

29. Briefly define and categorize the demographic transition.

_____

_____

_____

30. What is a population pyramid and what are the important contributions they provide to demographers?

_____

_____

_____

31. Describe several important push-and-pull factors of migration.

_____

_____

_____

_____

32. Provide several examples of forced migration.

_____

_____

_____

_____

33. Give some examples of environmental influence on population.

_____

_____

_____

_____

34. How does human perception play a role in distribution and settlement patterns?

_____

_____

_____

_____

35. Label and identify the various types of farm villages. How do isolated farmsteads differ?

_____
_____
_____
_____

CHAPTER FOUR

THE GEOGRAPHY OF LANGUAGE

Extended Chapter Outline (including key terms)

I. Linguistic Culture Regions
    Dialect, pidgin, creole, lingua franca, bilingualism, isoglosses, slang
    A. Language families
        1. Indo-European
        2. Sino-Tibetan
        3. Afro-Asiatic
        4. Others

II. Linguistic Diffusion
    A. Indo-European diffusion: Kurgan hypothesis
    B. Austronesian diffusion
    C. Language proliferation: one or many?

III. Linguistic Ecology
    A. Environment and vocabulary
    B. The environment helps shape language areas and guide migration
    C. The environment provides refuge: linguistic refuge areas

IV. Culturo-Linguistic Interaction
    A. Technology, language, and empire
    B. Language and cultural survival: language hotspots
    C. Religion and language

V. Linguistic Landscapes
    A. Messages and toponyms
    B. Generic toponyms of the United States
    C. Toponyms and cultures of the past

LEARNING OBJECTIVES

After reading this chapter *and* studying the maps and illustrations, you should be able to:

1. Explain and understand the difference between a language family, a language, a dialect, and a linguistic accent.

2. Describe the diffusion process of several major language families throughout the world.

3. Demonstrate the various relationships between language and the natural environment.

4. Discuss the influence of nature and cultural environment on languages.

5. Explain the roles of cultural diffusion and globalization involving language.

6. Understand the roles of language and religion.

7. Interpret the cultural landscape through the reading of various toponyms.

8. Grasp a better understanding of the place or region where you live by interpreting local toponyms.

SELECTED MAP READING AND INTERPRETATION

This section of the Study Guide is intended to heighten your map reading and interpretation skills. It will also help you apply the text readings to visual and spatial display of concepts, themes, and examples in human and cultural geography.

A world atlas (in print or online) will be very useful in completing this section of the Study Guide and will enhance your comprehension of the maps in the textbook. Ask your instructor to recommend an appropriate web site or atlas to purchase (or visit the map collection at your library). A world atlas is essential for your personal reference library, not only during this course, but throughout your college career.

After reading the text and then studying the accompanying map and its captions, answer the following questions.

FIGURE 4.1. Major linguistic formal culture regions of the world

1. What is the most widespread or spatially dominant language subgroup spoken on each continent? (It is important to know the boundary between Asia and Europe!)

_____

_____

_____

2. List five countries where the Austronesian language subgroup is spoken, including an African island state.

_____

_____

_____

3. Looking at this map, do you see the reason behind the name "Indo-European" family? Explain.

_____

_____

_____

4. Identify the language subgroup for the following independent countries: Vietnam, South Korea, Cameroon, Eritrea, Suriname, Hungary, Iceland, and Lebanon.

_____

_____

_____

FIGURE 4.6. Major dialects of North American English

1. What and where are the Missouri Apex and the Hoosier Apex?

_____

_____

_____

2. What dialects are spoken in Southern California, Kentucky, North Dakota, and most of Ohio? What do you think about this map? Is it correct in your opinion? Why or why not?

_____

_____

_____

3. What does this map tell you about culture, mobility, settlement, and history of the United States? Why is the "Southern" dialect so distinctive here?

_____

_____

_____

FIGURE 4.7. Origin and diffusion of four major language families in the Eastern Hemisphere

1. What present-day countries comprise the source area or hearth of the Niger-Congo language family?

_____

_____

_____

2. Where is the original source area of modern English?

_____

_____

_____

FIGURE 4.10 The environment is a linguistic refuge in the Caucasus Mountains

1. The past decade has witnessed a secessionist movement in the region of Chechnya. In which independent country is Chechnya located and what is the language family subgroup of the Chechen language?

_____

_____

_____

2. Can you determine an east-west spatial pattern among two of the language family subgroups? What is it?

_____

_____

_____

3. Does this map show greater diversity of languages at higher or lower elevations of terrain? (You will probably require an atlas to find the answer.) Can you explain the basis for the spatial patterns?

_____

_____

_____

4. Find the areas where Georgian and Ossetian are spoken. What does this tell you about the Russian-Georgian conflict in 2008? How is language a factor?

_____

_____

_____

FIGURE 4.19. Generic place-names reveal the migration of Yankee New Englanders

1. Study the map. Can you think of any reasons, historical or physical, why the areas of upstate New York and northern Maine are practically devoid of the place-name types indicated on this map?

_____

_____

_____

2. There is a concentration of typical place-name characteristics of New England found in northeastern Ohio. Can you think of any reasons for this concentration and why other areas of Ohio have far fewer of these toponyms?

_____

_____

_____

FIGURE 4.22. Arabic toponyms in Iberia

1. Using this map, speculate concerning the direction of the Moorish invasion and retreat, the duration of Moorish Islamic rule in different parts of Iberia, and the main centers of former Moorish power.

_____

_____

_____

2. Based on the text reading and using an atlas, list some present day place-names that you consider to be of Arabic origin.

_____

_____

_____

3. Look at the place-names on a map of your home state or province. Are any toponyms derived from languages other than English? (Perhaps from Spanish, French, or Native American languages?) What do these place-names reveal to you about the history of these regions?

_____

_____

_____

MATCHING EXERCISES

Match each key term from the text to its definition. Answers are found at the end of this Study Guide.

Set 1

_____ 1. bilingualism

a. A theory of language diffusion, which holds that the spread of Indo-European languages originated with animal domestication; originated in the central Asian steppes; and was later, more violent, and swifter than proponents of the Anatolian hypothesis maintain.

_____ 2. creole

b. A language derived from a pidgin language that has acquired a fuller vocabulary and become the native language of its speakers.

_____ 3. dialect

c. The border of usage of an individual word or pronunciation.

_____ 4. generic toponym

d. A distinctive local or regional variant of a language that remains mutually intelligible to speakers of other dialects of that language; a subtype of a language.

_____ 5. isogloss

e. The descriptive part of many place-names, often repeated throughout a culture area.

_____ 6. Kurgan hypothesis

f. The ability to speak two languages fluently.

Set 2

_____ 7. language

a. A group of related languages derived from a common ancestor.

_____ 8. language family

b. Those places on Earth that are home to the most unique, misunderstood, or endangered languages.

_____ 9. language hotspots

c. An area protected by isolation or inhospitable environmental conditions in which a language or dialect has survived.

_____ 10. lingua franca

d. A mutually agreed-on system of symbolic communication that has a spoken and usually a written expression.

_____ 11. linguistic refuge area

e. An existing, well-established language of communication and commerce used widely where it is not a mother tongue.

Set 3

_____ 12. pidgin

a. A composite language consisting of a small vocabulary borrowed from the linguistic groups involved in international commerce.

_____ 13. polyglot

b. A mixture of different languages.

_____ 14. slang

c. A place-name, usually consisting of two parts: the generic and the specific.

_____ 15. toponym

d. Words and phrases that are not part of a standard, recognized vocabulary for a given language but that are nonetheless used and understood by some of its speakers.

REVIEW: Self-evaluation Tests

PART ONE: Multiple-choice

Circle the best answer for each question. When you are finished, read each question again with your selected answer. After you are satisfied with your practice test, use the Answer Key in the back of the Study Guide to check your responses.

1. Languages can be defined as:
   a. speech patterns of various ethnic groups.
   b. tongues that can be mutually understood.
   c. speech patterns of singular ethnic groups.
   d. tongues that cannot be mutually understood.
   e. a collection of recognizable and similar dialects.

2. Approximately _____ languages are spoken in the world today.
   a. 850
   b. 1200
   c. 3000
   d. 4500
   e. 6000

3. One existing language may be elevated to the status of _____, or language of communication and commerce, over a wide area where it is not the mother tongue.
   a. pidgin language
   b. pidgin dialect
   c. lingua franca
   d. official or national language
   e. none of the above

4. The borders of individual word usage or pronunciations are called:
   a. linguistic culture regions.
   b. isoglosses.
   c. language dependency zones.
   d. language continuum.
   e. linguistic islands.

5. Languages in the Indo-European language family do NOT include:
   a. Turkish.
   b. German.
   c. Farsi (Persian).
   d. English.
   e. Romanian.

6. Three major languages of the Semitic people are Hebrew, Amharic, and:
   a. Farsi (Persian).
   b. Syrian.
   c. Turkish.
   d. Arabic.
   e. Greek.

7. Swahili, an important language of East Africa, is a member of what language family?
   a. Altaic
   b. Austronesia
   c. Nilo-Saharan
   d. Niger-Congo
   e. Khoisan

8. The earliest speakers of Indo-European apparently lived in what is now:
   a. India.
   b. Turkey.
   c. Russia.
   d. Germany.
   e. the Fertile Crescent.

9. The diffusion of which language family is strongly associated with island culture and vast expanses of ocean?
   a. Austronesian
   b. Indo-European
   c. Semitic
   d. Niger-Congo
   e. none of the above

10. The Spanish languages, derived from Castile, as well as the Celtic tongues, are especially rich in words describing rough terrain, such as mountains.
    a. True
    b. False

11. A good example of a linguistic refuge area is:
    a. Poland.
    b. Japan.
    c. southern India.
    d. South Africa.
    e. the Caucasus region.

12. Although physical barriers such as mountain ridges can slow groups from migrating from one place to another, they infrequently serve as linguistic borders.
    a. True
    b. False

13. The Treaty of Tordesillas divided _____ between Portuguese and Spanish control.
    a. Mexico
    b. the Caribbean realm
    c. South America
    d. Brazil
    e. Argentina

14. Which is not one of the top five most prevalent languages in the world?
    a. Japanese.
    b. English.
    c. Arabic.
    d. Chinese.
    e. French.

15. In Muslim lands such as parts of India, Bangladesh, and Indonesia, the language of religious ceremony is:
    a. the local language.
    b. the regional lingua franca.
    c. Dravidian, Bengali, and Malay.
    d. Arabic.
    e. Sanskrit.

16. Another term for place-names is:
    a. call signs.
    b. landscape symbols.
    c. toponyms.
    d. signage.
    e. none of the above

17. Many place-names consist of:
    a. generic parts.
    b. symbolic parts.
    c. specific parts.
    d. Both answers a and c are correct.
    e. none of the above

18. The place-name term "center" is frequently used in what American region?
    a. New England
    b. Deep South
    c. upper Midwest
    d. California
    e. Southwest

19. Most of the world's nearly extinct languages are found in:
    a. the Pacific realm.
    b. Asia.
    c. Africa.
    d. the Americas.
    e. Europe.

20. The remnants of descriptive Arabic place-names are commonly found in regions of:
   a. Italy.
   b. Greece.
   c. France.
   d. Spain.
   e. Hungary.

21. It is a fact that language is the basis for the expression of all elements of culture.
   a. True
   b. False

22. The native people of New Zealand are the:
   a. Maori.
   b. Aborigines.
   c. Austronesians.
   d. Micronesians.
   e. Moors.

PART TWO: Short-answer (probable essay-type questions)

23. Briefly list some of the major themes encompassed in the study of the geography of language.
   _____
   _____
   _____

24. What defines a language family and what are some examples?
   _____
   _____
   _____

25. List some of the language subfamilies of the Indo-European language family.
   _____
   _____
   _____

26. Briefly trace the origin and diffusion of the Indo-European language family.
   _____
   _____
   _____

27. What are some of the barriers to language diffusion?
   _____
   _____
   _____

28. What are the major regional dialects of the United States? Do you agree with these designations? Why or why not?

_____
_____
_____

29. Explain the diffusion of the languages of the Polynesian peoples, such as the Hawaiians, and why this diffusion merits special attention.

_____
_____
_____

30. What are the principal language families of Africa and the Middle East?

_____
_____
_____

31. Describe some of the relationships between the environment and vocabulary.

_____
_____
_____

32. How does language guide migration? Is this phenomenon true today? Why or why not?

_____
_____
_____

33. Provide some examples of both specific and generic toponyms.

_____
_____
_____

34. What are some place names in the United States derived from Native American, French, and Spanish languages? Can you think of other toponym origins in your local region?

_____
_____
_____

35. Briefly describe the various interactions between language and environment/habitat.

_____
_____
_____

CHAPTER FIVE

GEOGRAPHIES OF RACE AND ETHNICITY

Extended Chapter Outline (including key terms)

I. What Are Race and Ethnicity?
   A. Ethnicity, race, racism, ethnic groups
   B. Acculturation and assimilation
   C. Ethnic geography

II. Ethnic Regions
   A. Ethnic homelands and islands; ethnic substrates
   B. Ethnic neighborhoods and racialized ghettos; ethnoburbs
   C. Recent shifts in ethnic mosaics

III. Cultural Diffusion and Ethnicity
   A. Migration and ethnicity
      1. Chain migration
      2. Involuntary migration
      3. Ethnic cleansing
      4. Return migration and channelization
   B. Simplification and isolation

IV. Ethnic Ecology
   A. Cultural preadaptation and cultural maladaptation
   B. Habitat and the preservation of difference
   C. Environmental racism

V. Ethnic Cultural Interaction
   A. Ethnicity and business activity
   B. Ethnicity and type of employment
   C. Indigenous identities in the face of globalization

VI. Ethnic Landscapes
   A. Urban ethnic landscapes
   B. Re-creation of ethnic cultural landscapes
   C. Ethnic culinary landscapes: foodways

LEARNING OBJECTIVES

After reading this chapter *and* studying the maps and illustrations, you should be able to:

1. Present examples and explain how various groups define "ethnicity."

2. Understand the definitions of, and relationships between, national character, national origin, nationality, race, and ethnicity.

3. Discuss the process and characteristics of ethnic migration and mobility.

4. Discuss ethnic settlement patterns, cultural preadaptation, and ethnic survival.

5. Describe the cultural integration of ethnicity and livelihood, employment, and foodways.

6. Identify and describe elements of the ethnic landscape, including settlement patterns and urban landscapes.

7. Distinguish between an ethnic homeland and an ethnic island.

8. Understand the processes involving ethnicity and assimilation, acculturation, and re-awareness.

9. Begin to understand the role of ethnicity in your family, ancestors, and local neighborhood or region.

SELECTED MAP READING AND INTERPRETATION

This section of the Study Guide is intended to heighten your map reading and interpretation skills. It will also help you apply the text readings to visual and spatial display of concepts, themes, and examples in human and cultural geography.

A world atlas (in print or online) will be very useful in completing this section of the Study Guide and will enhance your comprehension of the maps in the textbook. Ask your instructor to recommend an appropriate web site or atlas to purchase (or visit the map collection at your library). A world atlas is essential for your personal reference library, not only during this course, but throughout your college career.

After reading the text and then studying the accompanying map and its captions, answer the following questions.

FIGURE 5.5. Ethnic minorities in China

1. Which of the ethnic regions are homelands and which are islands? How do you know?

   _____

   _____

   _____

2. Compare this to a map of population distribution in China. Why are China's ethnic groups concentrated in sparsely populated peripheries of the country?

   _____

   _____

   _____

3. Can you predict a breakup of the People's Republic of China, similar to the collapse and partition of the Soviet Union? Based on ethnicity, what new countries would you foresee?

   _____

   _____

   _____

4. Is this map an example of environmental racism? Why or why not?

   _____

   _____

   _____

FIGURE 5.7. Selected ethnic homelands in North America . . .

1. What are the viable ethnic homelands and why do you think they are considered viable?

   _____

   _____

   _____

2. What are some of the ethnic islands in the regions of ethnic island concentrations?

   _____

   _____

   _____

3. Because they are left blank, are states such as Kentucky without ethnicity? Why or why not?

   _____

   _____

   _____

4. Why are there no ethnic homelands indicated for Native Americans?

   _____

   _____

   _____

FIGURE 5.8. Ethnic and national-origin groups in North America

1. What is the specific Slavic ethnic group shown in Texas?

   _____

   _____

   _____

2. Where are the areas of Dutch ethnicity on the map?

   _____

   _____

   _____

3. Which state shows only "English" ethnicity?

   _____

   _____

   _____

4. Is there a relationship between the African ethnic area and the terrain or physical environment?

   _____

   _____

   _____

FIGURES 5.12, 5.13, 5.14, and 5.15. Maps of ethnicity in the United States

1. Compare these four maps. What patterns emerge? Do specific states share similar statistics?

    _____

    _____

    _____

2. Compare locations of Latino and Asian populations. What "state" patterns emerge? Why?

    _____

    _____

    _____

3. Name some reasons for the spatial patterns by state on these maps.

    _____

    _____

    _____

4. How do you think urbanization patterns in the United States affect ethnic patterns on these maps? Why? Explain.

    _____

    _____

    _____

    _____

FIGURE 5.20. Ethnic pluralities in the Caucasus

1. What is the relationship between ethnicity and physical terrain in this region?

    _____

    _____

    _____

2. Why do you think there are more ethnic groups in Russia than in Armenia, Georgia, and Azerbaijan?

    _____

    _____

    _____

3. Using additional sources, what can you determine about religion, language, and ethnicity in the Caucasus region? How does this impact politics and governments?

    _____

    _____

    _____

MATCHING EXERCISES

Match each key term from the text to its definition. Answers are found at the end of this Study Guide.

Set 1

_____ 1. acculturation

_____ 2. assimilation

_____ 3. chain migration

_____ 4. channelization

_____ 5. cultural maladaptation

_____ 6. cultural preadaptation

a. The complete blending of an ethnic group into the host society resulting in the loss of all distinctive ethnic traits.

b. The tendency of people to migrate along channels, over a period of time, from specific source areas to specific destinations.

c. Poor or inadequate adaptation that occurs when a group pursues an adaptive strategy that, in the short run, fails to provide the necessities of life or, in the long run, destroys the environment that nourishes it.

d. A complex of adaptive traits and skills possessed in advance of migration by a group, giving it survival ability and competitive advantage in occupying the new environment.

e. A migration process in which a specific source location becomes linked to a particular destination, so that neighbors in the old place become neighbors in the new place.

f. The adoption by an ethnic group of enough of the ways of the host society to be able to function economically and socially.

Set 2

_____ 7. cultural simplification

_____ 8. environmental racism

_____ 9. ethnic cleansing

_____ 10. ethnic flag

_____ 11. ethnic geography

_____ 12. ethnic group

a. The study of the spatial aspects of ethnicity.

b. The process by which immigrant ethnic groups lose certain aspects of their traditional culture in the process of settling overseas, creating a new culture that is less complex than the old.

c. The targeting of areas where ethnic or racial minorities live with respect to environmental contamination or failure to enforce environmental regulations.

d. A readily visible marker of ethnicity on the landscape.

e. The removal of unwanted ethnic minority populations from a nation-state through mass killing, deportation, or imprisonment.

f. A group of people who share a common ancestry and cultural tradition, often living as a minority group in a larger society.

Set 3

_____ 13. ethnic homeland

a. A small ethnic area in the rural countryside; sometimes called a "folk island."

_____ 14. ethnic island

b. A sizable area inhabited by an ethnic minority that exhibits a strong sense of attachment to the region and often exercises some measure of political and social control over it.

_____ 15. ethnic neighborhood

c. A suburban ethnic neighborhood, sometimes home to relatively affluent immigration populations.

_____ 16. ethnic substrate

d. A voluntary community where people of like origin reside by choice.

_____ 17. ethnoburb

e. Regional cultural distinctiveness that remains following the assimilation of an ethnic homeland.

Set 4

_____ 18. foodways

a. A type of ethnic diffusion that involves the voluntary movement of a group of migrants back to its ancestral or native country or homeland.

_____ 19. ghetto

b. The belief that human capabilities are determined by racial classification and that some races are superior to others.

_____ 20. involuntary migration

c. Customary behaviors associated with food preparation and consumption.

_____ 21. race

d. Traditionally, an area within a city where an ethnic group lives, either by choice or by force. Today in the United States, the term typically indicates an impoverished African-American urban neighborhood.

_____ 22. racism

e. A classification system that is sometimes understood as arising from genetically significant differences among human populations, or visible differences in human physiognomy, or as a social construction that varies across time and space.

_____ 23. return migration

f. Also called forced migration, refers to the forced displacement of a population, whether by government policy (such as a resettlement program), warfare or other violence, ethnic cleansing, disease, natural disaster, or enslavement.

REVIEW: Self-evaluation Tests

PART ONE: Multiple-choice

Circle the best answer for each question. When you are finished, read each question again with your selected answer. After you are satisfied with your practice test, use the Answer Key in the back of the Study Guide to check your responses.

1. The larger society in which an ethnic group resides is referred to as a(n):
    a. ethnic island.
    b. ethnic majority.
    c. host culture.
    d. national majority.
    e. none of the above

2. When an ethnic group adopts enough of the ways of the larger society to function, this is termed:
    a. assimilation.
    b. acculturation.
    c. cultural adaptation.
    d. preadaptation.
    e. melting pot.

3. A complete blending with the larger society by an ethnic group is termed:
    a. assimilation.
    b. acculturation.
    c. cultural adaptation.
    d. preadaptation.
    e. melting pot.

4. The main difference between ethnic islands and ethnic homelands is:
    a. location.
    b. spatial distribution.
    c. level of cultural integration.
    d. settlement patterns.
    e. size.

5. "Deseret" is a term used by some for the homeland of:
    a. Louisiana French.
    b. French Canadians.
    c. Mexican-Americans.
    d. Jewish-Americans.
    e. the Mormons.

6. Ethnic islands are much more numerous than homelands but as common as ethnic substrates.
   a. True
   b. False

7. A ghetto is traditionally defined as a certain urban quarter where:
   a. people are a racial minority.
   b. people are forced to live.
   c. people of a minority religion live.
   d. Jews traditionally live.
   e. none of the above

8. The most numerous ethnic minorities in North American cities today are originally from:
   a. Africa.
   b. India.
   c. Mexico.
   d. East Asia.
   e. former Communist lands.

9. When compared to the United States, which of the following ethnic or national origin groups is poorly represented in Canada?
   a. African
   b. Hispanic
   c. German
   d. Mexican
   e. all of the above

10. According to the text and tables, the largest national origin/ethnic group in the United States is:
    a. Irish.
    b. English.
    c. German.
    d. African.
    e. Italian.

11. In the country of Russia, only about 80 percent of the people are ethnically Russian.
    a. True
    b. False

12. About one-third of all Canadians claim single ancestry from this ancestry group.
    a. English
    b. French
    c. German
    d. Ukrainian
    e. Scottish

13. The decision for members of an ethnic group to migrate and the actual migration usually involves:
    a. hierarchical diffusion.
    b. contagious diffusion.
    c. relocation diffusion.
    d. chain migration.
    e. all of the above

14. When ethnic immigrants introduce their culture in a new land, a profound _____ occurs.
    a. prejudice
    b. cultural simplification
    c. channelization
    d. return migration
    e. all of the above

15. The example of Finnish settlement patterns in Wisconsin represents a case of:
    a. preadaptation.
    b. assimilation.
    c. adaptive strategy.
    d. first effective settlement.
    e. none of the above

16. President Barack Obama, Selena, and Tiger Woods are all examples of people of:
    a. color.
    b. Latino and Hispanic heritage.
    c. multiple races.
    d. dual nationality.
    e. ethnic assimilation.

17. The ecology of ethnic survival is often related to isolation and:
    a. language.
    b. religion.
    c. elevation.
    d. food.
    e. race.

18. Light blue is a Greek ethnic color, but in Chinese urban neighborhoods the venerated and auspicious color is:
    a. black.
    b. purple.
    c. green.
    d. red.
    e. yellow.

19. Green, a traditional color of ethnic Irish Catholics, is also found throughout the world in _____ neighborhoods.
    a. Japanese
    b. Russian
    c. Muslim
    d. Indian
    e. French

20. Terminology in ethnic studies is often confusing. For example, if a native white South African migrates to the United States, does he become an "African-American"? In this and many respects, definitions of ethnic identity are often ones of perception and self-recognition.
    a. True
    b. False

21. A striking, highly visible imprint on the land signifying and illustrating ethnicity is known as a(n):
    a. ethnic flag.
    b. ethnic substrate.
    c. mission of identity.
    d. cultural heritage landmark.
    e. re-creation of ethnic identity.

22. The American city with the highest percentage of a foreign-born population is:
    a. New York.
    b. Los Angeles.
    c. Seattle.
    d. Atlanta.
    e. Miami.

PART TWO: Short-answer (probable essay-type questions)

23. What are some of the cultural and ethnic features that make Wilbur, Nebraska, "The Czech Capital of Nebraska"?
    _____
    _____
    _____

24. Define the terms "ethnic group" and "host culture."
    _____
    _____
    _____

25. Explain the difference between acculturation and assimilation.

_____

_____

_____

26. What is the focus of ethnic geography studies?

_____

_____

_____

27. What are the two distinct geographical types of ethnic regions? Provide an example of each.

_____

_____

_____

28. Provide an example of an ethnic homeland and an ethnic island in North America.

_____

_____

_____

29. Explain the difference between an ethnic neighborhood and an ethnic ghetto.

_____

_____

_____

30. Why are cities in North America more ethnically diverse than any other urban centers in the world?

_____

_____

_____

31. What are the top five ethnic ancestry/national origin groups in the United States? How is this different from Canada?

_____

_____

_____

32. Explain the concept of chain migration.

_____

_____

_____

33. Briefly discuss the concept of preadaptation in ethnic migration.

_____

_____

_____

34. Provide some examples of ethnic environmental racism.

_____

_____

_____

35. What is the relationship between ethnicity and business activity?

_____

_____

_____

36. What is the relationship between ethnicity and type of employment?

_____

_____

_____

37. Who and where are the Hmong-Americans, and what are their distinctive gardening practices?

_____

_____

_____

38. What is an example of an "ethnic flag"?

_____

_____

_____

39. How can colors connote and reveal ethnicity? Provide examples.

_____

_____

_____

40. What are some local examples of ethnicity in your hometown, city, or region?

_____

_____

_____

41. Nearly everyone in North America is part of some ethnic fabric or identity. Describe the role of ethnicity or ethnic ancestry in your family or acquaintances.

_____

_____

_____

CHAPTER SIX

POLITICAL GEOGRAPHY

Extended Chapter Outline (including key terms)

I. Political Culture Regions
   A. A world of states
      1. Sovereignty
      2. Territoriality
      3. Colonialism
   B. Distribution of national territory
      1. Enclave, pene-enclave
      2. Exclave
   C. Boundaries
      1. Buffer state
      2. Satellite state
      3. Natural, ethnographic, geometric, and relic boundaries
   D. Spatial organization of territory
      1. Unitary state
      2. Federal state
   E. Centrifugal and centripetal forces; nationalism
   F. Supranational political bodies
      1. Regional trading blocs
      2. European Union
   G. Electoral geography: gerrymandering

II. Political Diffusion
   A. Core and periphery
   B. Diffusion and political innovation
   C. Politics and migration

III. Political Ecology
   A. Geopolitics and folk fortresses
   B. Heartland theory
   C. Warfare and environmental destruction

IV. Politico-Cultural Interaction
   A. The nation-state
   B. Ethnic separatism
   C. The cleavage model
   D. Political imprint on economic geography

V. Political Landscapes
   A. Imprint of the legal code
   B. Physical properties of boundaries
   C. The impress of central authority
   D. National iconography on the landscape

LEARNING OBJECTIVES

After reading this chapter *and* studying the maps and illustrations, you should be able to:

1. Describe various types of states, countries, and other political bodies.

2. Understand the themes and concepts associated with country building and borders.

3. Explain the political ecology of warfare and environmental destruction, the cleavage model, and Mackinder's heartland theory.

4. Explain the relationship of ethnicity and territory to the nation-state and the multinational and supranational state.

5. Describe the effects of political decision making on the cultural landscape.

6. Provide examples of the basic elements of the political landscape such as the boundary.

7. Better understand many of the world's current geopolitics, political conflicts, and wars, based on your knowledge of political and cultural geography.

SELECTED MAP READING AND INTERPRETATION

This section of the Study Guide is intended to heighten your map reading and interpretation skills. It will also help you apply the text readings to visual and spatial display of concepts, themes, and examples in human and cultural geography.

A world atlas (in print or online) will be very useful in completing this section of the Study Guide and will enhance your comprehension of the maps in the textbook. Ask your instructor to recommend an appropriate web site or atlas to purchase (or visit the map collection at your library). A world atlas is essential for your personal reference library, not only during this course, but throughout your college career.

After reading the text and then studying the accompanying map and its captions, answer the following questions.

FIGURE 6.1. The independent countries of the world

1. The United States basically shares a border with only two countries. How many countries now border Russia and what are they? (Don't forget Norway!)

    _____
    _____
    _____

2. What are the newly formed independent countries of central Asia and the Caucasus region that were formerly part of the Soviet Union?

    _____
    _____
    _____

3. What independent countries were derived from the breakup of Yugoslavia, Ethiopia, and Czechoslovakia in the 1990s?

    _____
    _____
    _____

4. Locate these independent countries on the world map:
    Bhutan, Sierra Leone, Oman, French Guiana, Slovenia, Lithuania, Belize, Papua New Guinea, Swaziland, Haiti, and Vanuatu

    _____
    _____
    _____
    _____

FIGURE 6.3. Two independent countries, A and B

1. These are real countries. Using an atlas, identify them. This may be challenging to some!

    _____
    _____

2. The conditions shown and described here are for 1994. What was the territorial outcome of this dispute?

_____

_____

_____

3. What and where are the actual religions, languages, and ethnicities of the various territories shown on this map?

_____

_____

_____

FIGURE 6.5. *Some supranational political organizations in the Eastern Hemisphere*

1. Can you identify the reasons why certain European countries, such as Norway, Switzerland, Albania, and Turkey, are *not* part of the European Union?

_____

_____

_____

2. Are all the member countries of the Arab League located in the Middle East? What is the status of the country between Morocco and Mauritania?

_____

_____

_____

3. What territories of the former Soviet Union are *not* part of the Commonwealth of Independent States? Why not?

_____

_____

_____

FIGURE 6.10. *Russia developed from a core area*

1. Can you think of reasons why expansion to the east was greater than to the west? What were the barriers?

_____

_____

_____

2. What environmental goals might have motivated Russian expansion?

_____

_____

_____

3. What were the causes behind the recent contraction of the country? Do you foresee any further contraction?

_____

_____

_____

FIGURE 6.11. *Independence from European or white minority rule*

1. Can you identify some barriers that slowed the diffusion of independence in Africa?

_____

_____

_____

2. 1960 was a landmark year for African independence. Using other maps, can you identify areas of British, French, Belgian, and Portuguese rule in Africa and show if a relationship exists between colonial ruler and year of independence?

_____

_____

_____

3. Why did independence come so late to Namibia? Can you find any reasons for this? Who were the colonial rulers of Namibia?

_____

_____

_____

4. List all the countries achieving independence before 1960 and their respective year of sovereignty. (Also identify the Arab countries included here.)

_____

_____

_____

FIGURE 6.16. *Nation-states, multinational countries, and other types*

1. Identify 10 nation-states from this map.

_____

_____

_____

2. Why are the countries of Great Britain and Spain classified as old multinational states?

_____

_____

_____

3. What is your opinion on the United States as a country evolving toward nation-statehood?

_____

_____

_____

4. This classification of nation-state is arbitrary and debatable. How would you change it, and why?

_____

_____

_____

FIGURE 6.19. Kurdistan

1. In what countries are areas of Kurdish predominance found?

_____

_____

_____

2. Using your atlas, can you identify the physical landscape of Kurdistan and thus show that a folk fortress situation exists?

_____

_____

_____

3. Why and how does this map show reasons for political instability in this region? Is this especially true for Iraq and Iran? Why or why not?

_____

_____

_____

4. If Kurdistan become an independent country, what problems of a geopolitical nature, such as access to the seas, may it experience?

_____

_____

_____

MATCHING EXERCISES

Match each key term from the text to its definition. Answers are found at the end of this Study Guide.

Set 1

_____ 1. buffer state

a. The territorial nucleus from which a country grows in area and over time, often containing the national capital and the main center of commerce, culture, and industry.

_____ 2. centrifugal force

b. The building and maintaining of colonies in one territory by people based elsewhere.

_____ 3. centripetal force

c. A political-geographic model suggesting that persistent regional patterns in voting behavior, sometimes leading to separatism, can usually be explained in terms of tensions pitting urban against rural, core against periphery, capitalists against workers, and power group against minority culture.

_____ 4. cleavage model

d. Any factor that supports the internal unity of a country.

_____ 5. colonialism

e. Any factor that disrupts the internal order of a country.

_____ 6. core area

f. An independent but small and weak country lying between two powerful countries.

Set 2

_____ 7. enclave

a. The study of the interactions among space, place, and region and the conduct and results of elections.

_____ 8. electoral geography

b. A political boundary that follows some cultural border, such as a linguistic or religious border.

_____ 9. ethnographic boundary

c. A piece of territory surrounded by, but not part of, a country.

_____ 10. European Union (EU)

d. A piece of national territory separated from the main body of a country by the territory of another country.

_____ 11. exclave

e. An independent country that gives considerable powers and even autonomy to its constituent parts.

_____ 12. federal state

f. A regional trading bloc composed of 27 European nations.

Set 3

_____ 13. folk fortress

a. The drawing of electoral district boundaries in an awkward pattern to enhance the voting impact of one constituency at the expense of another.

_____ 14. geometric boundary

b. A political border drawn in a regular, geometric manner, often a straight line, without regard for environmental or cultural patterns.

_____ 15. geopolitics

c. A stronghold area with natural defensive qualities, useful in the defense of a country against invaders.

74

_____ 16. gerrymandering

_____ 17. heartland

d. A 1904 proposal by Mackinder that the key to world conquest lay in control of the interior of Eurasia.

e. The interior of a sizable landmass, removed from maritime connections; in particular, the interior of the Eurasian continent.

_____ 18. heartland theory

f. The influence of the habitat on political entities.

Set 4

_____ 19. nationalism

a. An independent country dominated by a relatively homogeneous culture group.

_____ 20. nation-state

b. A political border that follows some feature of the natural environment, such as a river or mountain ridge.

_____ 21. natural boundary

c. The sense of belonging to and self-identification with a national culture.

_____ 22. political geography

d. A former political border that no longer functions as a boundary.

_____ 23. regional trading blocs

e. Agreements made among geographically proximate countries that reduce trade barriers in order to better compete with other regional markets.

_____ 24. relic boundary

f. The geographic study of politics and political matters.

Set 5

_____ 25. rimland

a. A small, weak country dominated by one powerful neighbor to the extent that some or much of its independence is lost.

_____ 26. satellite state

b. The maritime fringe of a country or continent; in particular, the western, southern, and eastern edges of the Eurasian continent.

_____ 27. sovereignty

c. The right of individual states to control political and economic affairs within their territorial boundaries without external interference.

_____ 28. state

d. Occurs when states willingly relinquish some degree of sovereignty in order to gain the benefits of belonging to a larger political-economic entity.

_____ 29. supranationalism

e. A centralized authority that enforces a single political, economic, and legal system within its territorial boundaries. Often used synonymously with "country."

Set 6

_____ 30. supranational organization

a. A group of independent countries joined together for purposes of mutual interest.

_____ 31. territoriality

b. A learned cultural response, rooted in European history, that produced the external bounding and internal territorial organization characteristic of modern states.

_____ 32. unitary state

c. An independent state that concentrates power in the central government and grants little authority to the provinces.

REVIEW: Self-evaluation Tests

PART ONE: Multiple-choice
Circle the best answer for each question. When you are finished, read each question again with your selected answer. After you are satisfied with your practice test, use the Answer Key in the back of the Study Guide to check your responses.

1. The Earth's surface is divided into approximately _____ independent countries.
    a. 230
    b. 320
    c. 280
    d. 200
    e. 190

2. Europe and Africa each have about the same number of independent countries.
    a. True
    b. False

3. Theoretically, the most desirable shape for a country is:
    a. elongated.
    b. square.
    c. hexagonal.
    d. triangular.
    e. none of the above

4. Which of the following are areas of national territory separated from the main body of a country by the territory of another?
    a. peninsulas
    b. exclaves
    c. enclaves
    d. colonies
    e. protectorates

5. Until quite recently, many boundaries were not clear or sharp, but undefined, somewhat fuzzy zones called:
    a. buffer states.
    b. frontiers.
    c. hinterlands.
    d. marchlands.
    e. international zones.

6. Mongolia and Nepal serve as good examples of:

    a. "shoestring" countries.
    b. buffer states.
    c. secessionist states.
    d. satellite states.
    e. rump or truncated states.

7. Boundaries that are based on neither cultural nor physical features are often:
   a. ethnographic.
   b. geometric.
   c. natural.
   d. irregular.
   e. none of the above

8. An excellent example of a relic boundary exists:
   a. between Canada and Alaska.
   b. between Brazil and Argentina.
   c. between Laos and Cambodia.
   d. within Germany.
   e. within Ireland.

9. A federal government is usually considered a less geographically expressive system.
   a. True
   b. False

10. The United States, Canada, France, and Australia are all examples of federal governments.
    a. True
    b. False

11. Whatever disrupts internal order and encourages destruction of the country is called:
    a. raison d'être.
    b. insurgency.
    c. centrifugal force.
    d. nationalism.
    e. centripetal force.

12. Electoral geography is useful for identifying:
    a. the Lower South.
    b. formal and functional culture regions.
    c. spatial patterns of ethnicity.
    d. supranational organizations.
    e. none of the above

13. The creation of districts that have a majority of voters favoring the group in power and a minority of opposition voters is called:
    a. gerrymandering.
    b. cleavage control districts.
    c. redistricting.
    d. raison d'être.
    e. selective electoral districts.

14. During political diffusion, the original core area seldom remains the country's most important district.
    a. True
    b. False

15. The Russian state originated in the small principality of:
    a. St. Petersburg.
    b. Kiev.
    c. Warsaw.
    d. Novgorad.
    e. Moscow.

16. Potentially, countries without political core areas, such as Zaire and Belgium, are the least stable of all independent states.
    a. True
    b. False

17. The best example of contagious expansion diffusion in political geography is:
    a. the growth of the Russian Empire.
    b. political independence in Africa.
    c. the creation of Mexico.
    d. British colonization of India.
    e. the reunification of Germany.

18. Throughout much of history, a country's survival was enhanced by some sort of natural protection. These areas of protection are called:
    a. national moats.
    b. natural defenses.
    c. ethnic islands.
    d. national shields.
    e. folk fortresses.

19. The "heartland theory" was developed by geographer:
    a. Wilbur Zelinsky.
    b. Hubert Wilhelm.
    c. Halford Mackinder.
    d. Stanley Brunn.
    e. Derwent Whittlesey.

20. The "heartland theory" predicted, in effect:
    a. the growth of southern Democrats.
    b. the economic power of the Midwest.
    c. the rise of French and British colonialism.
    d. Russian conquest of the world.
    e. Communism in mainland China.

21. Which of the following is NOT an example of a modern nation-state?
    a. Sweden
    b. Belgium
    c. Japan
    d. Armenia
    e. Germany

22. The greatest concentration of the francophone cultural-linguistic minority in Canada is found in:
   a. Toronto.
   b. Ontario.
   c. Manitoba.
   d. Newfoundland and New Brunswick.
   e. Quebec.

23. The "impress of central authority" refers to:
   a. usually unitary rather than federal states.
   b. transportation networks.
   c. omnipresent military authority.
   d. government and landscape.
   e. none of the above

24. A good example of national iconography in the American landscape is:
   a. bald eagles and flags.
   b. the National Cathedral.
   c. the Grand Canyon.
   d. New York City.
   e. baseball.

PART TWO: Short answer (probable essay-type questions)

25. Briefly explain the process of contagious expansion diffusion by using the example of political independence in Africa.

   _____
   _____
   _____

26. What are folk fortresses and are they significant today?

   _____
   _____
   _____

27. Briefly summarize the importance of the heartland theory.

   _____
   _____
   _____

28. What are some of the environmental catastrophes associated with the Iraq War?

   _____
   _____
   _____

29. What is the difference between a nation-state and a multinational country? Use examples from each.

_____

_____

30. Briefly explain the cleavage model in political geography.

_____

_____

_____

31. How is the legal code imprinted on landscapes? Use examples.

_____

_____

_____

32. Describe the various types of boundaries between and within countries.

_____

_____

_____

33. What is some of the local political iconography of your state, province, or region?

_____

_____

_____

34. Define the term "territoriality."

_____

_____

_____

35. Provide some examples and explain the difference between exclaves and enclaves.

_____

_____

_____

36. Briefly describe and explain the difference between unitary and federal spatial organization of government.

_____

_____

_____

37. How and why are political boundaries barriers to cultural diffusion?

_____

_____

_____

38. State some of the contributions of geographer Halford Mackinder.

_____

_____

_____

CHAPTER SEVEN

THE GEOGRAPHY OF RELIGION

Extended Chapter Outline (including key terms)

I.   Classifying Religions
   A. Proselytic, universalizing, and ethnic religions
   B. Monotheism and polytheism
   C. Syncretic and orthodox religions
   D. Religious fundamentalism

II. Religious Culture Regions
   A. Judaism
   B. Christianity
      1. Western and Eastern
      2. Catholicism, Protestantism, Orthodoxy
   C. Islam
      1. Shiite
      2. Sunni
   D. Hinduism
   E. Buddhism
   F. Taoic Religions
   G. Animism/Shamanism

III. Religion Diffusion
   A. The Semitic religious hearth
   B. The Indus-Ganges hearth
   C. The East Asian religious hearth
   D. Barriers and time-distance decay

IV. Religious Ecology
   A. Appeasing the forces of nature; geomancy
   B. Ecotheology; teleology

V. Cultural Interaction in Religion
   A. Religion and economy
   B. Religious pilgrimage
   C. Religion, political geography, and the rise of
      Evangelical Protestantism in Latin America
   D. Relevance in a global world

VI. Religious Landscapes
   A. Religious structures
   B. Faithful details
   C. Landscapes of the dead
   D. Sacred space
   E. Religious names on the land

LEARNING OBJECTIVES

After reading this chapter *and* studying the maps and illustrations, you should be able to:

1. Understand and describe the origin and diffusion of major world religions and their subdivisions.

2. Explain why certain religions, such as Islam, expanded over several continents while other religions experienced little change in range or membership size.

3. Know and describe the difference between ethnic and proselytic religions. You should also know several examples from each type.

4. Understand the regional patterns of various branches of Christianity, especially in the United States.

5. Begin to understand the role of religion in shaping politics and the economy, especially in regard to territory.

6. Discuss the major theories explaining why three major monotheistic faiths (Islam, Judaism, and Christianity) began in the same geographic region, as well as the connections between these religions.

7. Understand the various relationships between the modification of the environment and different religions.

8. Discuss aspects and locations of animistic belief systems, including their attachment to the local natural world.

9. Interpret different burial systems and the resulting landscapes of the dead.

10. Begin to think about the role of religion in shaping the history, migration, settlement patterns, and cultural geography of your home region and perhaps your family and/or ancestors.

SELECTED MAP READING AND INTERPRETATION

This section of the Study Guide is intended to heighten your map reading and interpretation skills. It will also help you apply the text readings to visual and spatial display of concepts, themes, and examples in human and cultural geography.

A world atlas (in print or online) will be very useful in completing this section of the Study Guide and will enhance your comprehension of the maps in the textbook. Ask your instructor to recommend an appropriate Website or atlas to purchase (or visit the map collection at your library). A world atlas is essential for your personal reference library, not only during this course, but throughout your college career.

After reading the text and then studying the accompanying map and its captions, answer the following questions.

FIGURE 7.2. The world distribution of major religions

1. Other than some African countries, where is animism evident in the world?

   _____
   _____
   _____

2. What are the primarily Protestant countries of Europe?

   _____
   _____
   _____

3. Is Hinduism limited to India? If not, where else is it found?

   _____
   _____
   _____

4. Describe the changes in major religions of Africa from north to south.

   _____
   _____
   _____

FIGURE 7.3. Distribution of religious groups in Lebanon

1. What are the patterns of religious groups in Lebanon?

   _____
   _____
   _____

2. Can you think of reasons why Lebanon serves as a religious refuge area? What is the pattern of the physical terrain?

_____

_____

_____

3. Explain the differences among the three branches of Christianity found in Lebanon.

_____

_____

_____

FIGURE 7.6. *Leading Christian denominations in the United States and Canada*

1. Can you explain the patterns of religion in Texas and Louisiana?

_____

_____

_____

2. Why do you think that Lutheranism is most prevalent in the Upper Midwest?

_____

_____

_____

3. Can you explain why some states, such as Ohio, have no denominational majority, while others such as Utah and Mississippi have basically one majority?

_____

_____

_____

4. Other than Catholic, Baptist, and Lutheran majority areas, what other regional patterns are evident?

_____

_____

_____

5. Where is a Mennonite majority located? Does this include the Amish people, too?

_____

_____

_____

FIGURE 7.13. The diffusion of Christianity in Europe, first to eleventh centuries

1. Look at the patterns of diffusion by the year 300. In what way do these patterns suggest hierarchical expansion diffusion?

   _____
   _____
   _____

2. What barriers to diffusion might account for the uneven advance of Christianity by the year 1050?

   _____
   _____
   _____

3. What were the last "pagan" countries of Europe? They were not Christianized until the late fourteenth century.

   _____
   _____
   _____

FIGURE 7.19. Consumption and avoidance of pork are influenced by religion

1. Can you explain the pattern in the United States? Think of factors of economy and culture.

   _____
   _____
   _____

2. How do these global patterns correspond to the map (Figure 7.2) of major world religions?

   _____
   _____
   _____

FIGURE 7.24. Secularized areas in Europe

1. Look at German-speaking countries (Austria, Germany, Switzerland, Liechtenstein). What patterns prevail in secularization? Can you identify an east-west and/or north-south pattern?

   _____
   _____
   _____

2. Can you account for any reasons or similarities among regions where religion is most highly practiced?

   _____
   _____
   _____

MATCHING EXERCISES

Match each key term from the text to its definition. Answers are found at the end of this Study Guide.

Set 1

____ 1. animist

a. An adherent of animism, the idea that souls or spirits exist not only in humans but also in animals, plants, rocks, natural phenomena such as thunder, geographic features such as mountains or rivers, or other entities of the natural environment.

____ 2. contact conversion

b. A movement to return to the founding principles of a religion, which can include literal interpretation of sacred texts, or the attempt to follow the ways of a religious founder as closely as possible.

____ 3. culture hearth

c. The spread of religious beliefs by personal contact.

____ 4. ecotheology

d. A religion identified with a particular ethnic or tribal group; does not seek converts.

____ 5. ethnic religion

e. A focused geographic area where important innovations are born and from which they spread.

____ 6. fundamentalism

f. The study of the influence of religious belief on habitat modification.

Set 2

____ 7. monotheistic religion

a. A strand within most major religions that emphasizes purity of faith and is not open to blending with other religions.

____ 8. orthodox religion

b. A social system involving a set of beliefs and practices through which people seek harmony with the universe and attempt to influence the forces of nature, life, and death.

____ 9. pilgrimage

c. The worship of only one god.

____ 10. polytheistic religion

d. A journey to a place of religious importance.

____ 11. proselytic religion

e. The worship of many gods.

____ 12. religion

f. A religion that actively seeks new members and aims to convert all humankind.

Set 3

____ 13. sacred space

a. Also called a proselytic religion, it expands through active conversion of new members and aims to encompass all of humankind.

____ 14. syncretic religion

b. The belief that Earth was created especially for human beings, who are separate from and superior to the natural world.

____ 15. teleology

c. An area recognized by a religious group as worthy of devotion, loyalty, esteem, or fear to the extent that it becomes sought out, avoided, inaccessible to the nonbeliever, and/or removed from economic use.

____ 16. universalizing religion

d. A religion, or strand within a religion, that combines elements of two or more belief systems.

REVIEW: Self-evaluation Tests

PART ONE: Multiple-choice

Circle the best answer for each question. When you are finished, read each question again with your selected answer. After you are satisfied with your practice test, use the Answer Key in the back of the Study Guide to check your responses.

1. Religion can be defined as:
   a. cultural theory.
   b. a set of beliefs.
   c. worship of either one or many gods.
   d. a way of life.
   e. a form of organized cult.

2. Religions that seek new members are termed:
   a. aggressive.
   b. growth active.
   c. proselytic.
   d. charismatic.
   e. ethnic religions.

3. Judaism and Hinduism may be termed:
   a. aggressive.
   b. growth active.
   c. proselytic.
   d. charismatic.
   e. ethnic religions.

4. An example of sacred space is:
   a. Dome of the Rock.
   b. a Christian church.
   c. the Wailing Wall.
   d. all of the above
   e. none of the above

5. Islam may be termed a(n) _____ faith.
   a. polytheistic
   b. vernacular
   c. monotheistic
   d. ethnic
   e. none of the above

6. Christian Egyptians are often members of the Eastern group of Christianity called:
   a. the Coptic Church.
   b. Maronites.
   c. Eastern Orthodox.
   d. Melkites.
   e. Nestorians.

7. Most of the Christians of the highland region of Lebanon are:
   a. Copts.
   b. Nestorians.
   c. Greek Orthodox.
   d. Maronites.
   e. Presbyterians.

8. The core of the Latter Day Saints realm is:
   a. Nevada.
   b. Missouri.
   c. South Dakota.
   d. North Dakota.
   e. Utah.

9. Which of the following is considered a prophet of Islam?
   a. Jesus
   b. Moses
   c. Muhammad
   d. Abraham
   e. all of the above

10. The stronghold of the Shiite branch of Islam is the country of:
    a. Iraq.
    b. Iran.
    c. Saudi Arabia.
    d. Kuwait.
    e. Libya.

11. The Jews who eventually settled in central and eastern Europe were known as the:
    a. Ashkenazim.
    b. Orthodox.
    c. Hasidic.
    d. Sephardim.
    e. none of the above

12. The majority of the world's Jewish population lives in:
    a. Europe.
    b. Israel.
    c. Russia.
    d. North America.
    e. Poland and Romania.

13. The concept of "ahimsa" is focused on the:
    a. caste system.
    b. Dravidian ethnic divide.
    c. idea of nirvana.
    d. veneration of all life forms.
    e. Five Pillars of Islam.

14. Hinduism has splintered into diverse religious groups that are usually regarded as separate religions. Two major direct splinter groups are:
    a. Lamaism and Sikhism.
    b. Taoism and Lamaism.
    c. Coptic and Nestorian.
    d. Sikhism and Jainism.
    e. none of the above

15. Buddhism is a religion derived from Taoism.
    a. True
    b. False

16. Lamaism prevails not only in Tibet, but also in:
    a. Nepal.
    b. Mongolia.
    c. China.
    d. Thailand.
    e. all of the above

17. People who are considered _____ in their form of faith believe that rocks, rivers, and other natural features can possess spirits or souls.
    a. monotheistic
    b. theocratic
    c. animistic
    d. secularized
    e. heathen

18. The youngest religion of the Semitic religious hearth is:
    a. Islam.
    b. Judaism.
    c. Hinduism.
    d. Christianity.
    e. Sikhism.

19. The use of missionaries primarily involves the concept of:
    a. hierarchical diffusion.
    b. relocation diffusion.
    c. distance-decay.
    d. eminent domain.
    e. all of the above

20. When political leaders (such as kings) were converted to Christianity and their subjects later followed, the process of religious diffusion was termed:
    a. hierarchical diffusion.
    b. relocation diffusion.
    c. distance-decay.
    d. eminent domain.
    e. all of the above

21. Buddhism, although strongly associated with lands and people of southeastern and eastern Asia such as China and Laos, actually began in the Indian subcontinent.
    a. True
    b. False

22. Many followers of Islam make religious pilgrimages to the holy cities of Mecca and:
    a. Jiddah.
    b. Riyadh.
    c. Damascus.
    d. Cairo.
    e. Medina.

PART TWO: Short-answer (probable essay-type questions)

23. Provide examples of each and discuss the difference between proselytic and ethnic religions.
    _____
    _____
    _____

24. What are some of the general spatial patterns of religion in North America?
    _____
    _____
    _____

25. What are some of the characteristics of the Islamic faith?
    _____
    _____
    _____

26. What is polytheism and what are some examples of this form of religion?
    _____
    _____
    _____

27. Briefly discuss the origin and diffusion of Buddhism, including its fusion with native ethnic religions.
    _____
    _____
    _____

28. What are some common characteristics of animism and where can it be found today?
    _____
    _____
    _____

29. Briefly discuss theories regarding the origin of religions in the Semitic religious hearth.
    _____
    _____
    _____

30. Provide examples of the mobility of religion.

_____
_____
_____

31. What religions grew out of the Indus-Ganges religious hearth?

_____
_____
_____

32. What are some barriers in the diffusion of religion?

_____
_____
_____

33. What are the practices of ecotheology and how do they relate to the physical environment?

_____
_____
_____

34. What is the religious significance of Mount Shasta in California?

_____
_____
_____

35. How are environmental factors used to explain the origin of monotheistic faiths?

_____
_____
_____

36. Explain the "spiritual landscape."

_____
_____
_____

37. How can religion influence people's perception of the environment?

_____
_____
_____

38. Explain the use of fish and wine in Christianity as examples of the relationship between religion and economy.

_____
_____
_____

39. What are the various food taboos among Hindus, Muslims, Mormons, and Jews?

_____

_____

_____

40. What is the purpose of a religious pilgrimage and what are some very important pilgrimage sites for Jews, Muslims, and Christians?

_____

_____

_____

41. How do cemeteries preserve truly ancient cultural traits? Provide some examples.

_____

_____

_____

CHAPTER EIGHT

AGRICULTURE

Extended Chapter Outline (including key terms)

I. Agricultural Regions
   A. Swidden (shifting) cultivation
   B. Paddy rice farming, double-cropping
   C. Peasant grain, root, and livestock farming
   D. Plantation agriculture
   E. Market gardening
   F. Livestock fattening, feedlots
   G. Grain farming, suitcase farming, and agribusiness
   H. Dairying
   I. Nomadic herding vs. sedentary cultivation
   J. Livestock ranching
   K. Urban agriculture
   L. Farming the waters: aquaculture, mariculture
   M. Nonagricultural areas (hunting and gathering)

II. Agricultural Diffusion
   A. Origins and diffusion of plant domestication
   B. Locating centers of domestication
   C. Tracing animal domestication
   D. Exploration, colonialism, and the green revolution
   E. Labor mobility

III. Agricultural Ecology
   A. Cultural adaptation: nature and technology
   B. Sustainable agriculture
   C. Intensity of land use and desertification
   D. Environmental perception by agriculturists
   E. Organic agriculture and green fuels (biofuels)

IV. Cultural Interaction in Agriculture
   A. Agriculture and the economy: Local-global food provisioning
   B. Agriculture and transportation costs: the von Thünen model
   C. Can the world be fed?
   D. Globalization and the growth of agribusiness: monoculture, genetically modified crops
   E. Food fears

V. Agricultural Landscapes
   A. Survey, cadastral, and field patterns; hamlets
   B. Fencing
   C. Hedging

LEARNING OBJECTIVES

After reading this chapter *and* studying the maps and illustrations, you should be able to:

1. Describe various forms of agriculture such as subsistence agriculture and commercial livestock fattening.

2. Trace the origin and places of plant and animal domestication.

3. Discuss the contributions of several important scholars, including von Thünen, to the study of agriculture.

4. Explain and understand the diffusion of agriculture from one region or continent to another.

5. Describe the influence of the environment upon agricultural practices and how humans modify the earth to suit their agricultural needs and methods.

6. Understand and explain the role of human and environmental perception upon land use and agricultural production.

7. Discuss the effects of globalization and genetically modified (GM) crops on feeding the world.

8. Provide examples from around the world of various agricultural lifestyles and practices.

9. Understand the various techniques of land survey, land division, fencing, and hedging that shape the cultural landscape.

10. Continue to sharpen your skills in map reading and interpretation.

SELECTED MAP READING AND INTERPRETATION

This section of the Study Guide is intended to heighten your map reading and interpretation skills. It will also help you apply the text readings to visual and spatial display of concepts, themes, and examples in human and cultural geography.

A world atlas (in print or online) will be very useful in completing this section of the Study Guide and will enhance your comprehension of the maps in the textbook. Ask your instructor to recommend an appropriate web site or atlas to purchase (or visit the map collection at your library). A world atlas is essential for your personal reference library, not only during this course, but throughout your college career.

After reading the text and then studying the accompanying map and its captions, answer the following questions.

FIGURE 8.1. Agricultural regions of the world

1. What is the agricultural region stretching from France to Siberia and in what other areas of the world is it found?

   _____

   _____

   _____

2. Identify several regions and countries that are dominated by livestock fattening.

   _____

   _____

   _____

3. In which regions of the world is plantation agriculture practiced? Can you think of any reason why?

   _____

   _____

   _____

4. What agricultural regions are shared by Peru, Burkina Faso, Iraq, and North Korea?

   _____

   _____

FIGURE 8.4. Two agricultural regions in China

1. Where would you draw the cultural boundary between the two types of agriculture and what may account for this north-south pattern?

   _____

   _____

   _____

FIGURE 8.13. Global aquaculture and fisheries

1. In addition to China and India, what are the leading countries in aquaculture production?

    _____

    _____

    _____

2. Why do you think Australia ranks so low despite having a significant coastline? What other countries are low in production? Why?

    _____

    _____

    _____

FIGURE 8.14. Ancient centers of plant domestication

1. What are the reasons why this map should be regarded as theoretical or speculative?

    _____

    _____

2. What is the historic name of the region acknowledged as the hearth area of the earliest plant and animal domestication in the Middle Eastern region? Do some research.

    _____

    _____

    _____

3. Where are the regions of domestication of plants in the Americas? What vegetables were domesticated here and what was their possible path of diffusion?

    _____

    _____

    _____

FIGURE 8.19. Risk of desertification in Africa

1. What countries are facing the most severe desertification?

    _____

    _____

    _____

2. Using other maps, identify the general climate types, wind patterns, and topography in the three divisions of desertification on this map.

    _____

    _____

    _____

3. What contrasting rainfall regions exist in the yellow areas of this map? Why is desertification not a problem in many areas of the Sahara as well as the rainforest of the Congo Basin?

_____

_____

_____

FIGURE 8.23. *Ideal and actual distribution of types of agriculture in Uruguay*

1. In what ways does the spatial pattern of Uruguayan agriculture conform to von Thünen's model?

_____

_____

_____

2. How is the pattern of agriculture different from von Thünen's model and what might cause the anomalies?

_____

_____

_____

FIGURE 8.24. *Mapping hunger worldwide*

1. What geographic patterns does this map reveal?

_____

_____

_____

2. Can you explain the pattern in Africa? Why do you think North Africa (in the same category as the United States) is different from other regions of Africa?

_____

_____

_____

MATCHING EXERCISES

Match each key term from the text to its definition. Answers are found at the end of this Study Guide.

Set 1

____ 1. agribusiness

____ 2. agricultural landscape

____ 3. agricultural region

____ 4. agriculture

____ 5. aquaculture

a. The cultivation, under controlled conditions, of aquatic organisms primarily for food but also for scientific and aquarium uses.

b. The cultivation of domesticated crops and the raising of domesticated animals.

c. Highly mechanized, large-scale farming, usually under corporate ownership.

d. A geographic region defined by a distinctive combination of physical environmental conditions; crop type; settlement patterns; and labor, cultivation, and harvesting practices.

e. The cultural landscape of agricultural areas.

Set 2

____ 6. biofuel

____ 7. cadastral pattern

____ 8. cool chain

____ 9. desertification

____ 10. domesticated animal

____ 11. domesticated plant

____ 12. double-cropping

a. Broadly, this refers to any form of energy derived from biological matter, increasingly used in reference to replacements for fossil fuels in internal combustion engines, industrial processes, and the heating and cooling of buildings.

b. The shapes formed by property borders; the pattern of land ownership.

c. Harvesting twice a year from the same parcel of land.

d. A plant deliberately planted and tended by humans that is genetically distinct from its wild ancestors as a result of selective breeding.

e. The refrigeration and transport technologies that allow for the distribution of perishables.

f. A process whereby human actions unintentionally turn productive lands into deserts through agricultural and pastoral misuse, destroying vegetation and soil to the point where they cannot regenerate.

g. An animal kept for some utilitarian purpose whose breeding is controlled by humans and whose survival is dependent on humans.

Set 3

_____ 13. feedlot

a. Plants whose genetic characteristics have been altered through recombinant DNA technology.

_____ 14. genetically modified (GM) crops

b. A factorylike farm devoted to either livestock fattening or dairying; all feed is imported and no crops are grown on the farm.

_____ 15. green revolution

c. The recent introduction of high-yield hybrid crops and chemical fertilizers and pesticides into traditional Asian agricultural systems, most notably paddy rice farming, with attendant increases in production and ecological damage.

_____ 16. hamlet

d. A small rural settlement, smaller than a village.

_____ 17. hunting and gathering

e. The killing of wild game and the harvesting of wild plants to provide food in traditional cultures.

Set 4

_____ 18. intensive agriculture

a. Farming devoted to specialized fruit, vegetable, or vine crops for sale rather than consumption.

_____ 19. intercropping

b. A branch of aquaculture specific to the cultivation of marine organisms, often involving the transformation of coastal environments and the production of distinctive new landscapes.

_____ 20. livestock fattening

c. The expenditure of much labor and capital on a piece of land to increase its productivity. In contrast, _extensive_ agriculture involves less labor and capital.

_____ 21. mariculture

d. A commercial type of agriculture that produces fattened cattle and hogs for meat.

_____ 22. market gardening

e. The practice of growing two or more different types of crops in the same field at the same time. Also called _intertillage._

Set 5

_____ 23. monoculture

a. A member of a group that continually moves with its livestock in search of forage for its animals.

_____ 24. nomadic livestock herder

b. The raising of only one crop on a huge tract of land in agribusiness.

_____ 25. organic agriculture

c. A farmer belonging to a folk culture and practicing a traditional system of agriculture.

_____ 26. paddy rice farming

d. A form of farming that relies on manuring, mulching, and biological pest control and rejects the use of synthetic fertilizers, insecticides, herbicides, and genetically modified crops.

_____ 27. peasant

e. The cultivation of rice on a paddy, or small flooded field, practiced in the humid areas of the Far East.

Set 6

____ 28. plantation

a. Farming to supply the minimum food and materials necessary to survive.

____ 29. plantation agriculture

b. A large landholding devoted to specialized production of a tropical cash crop.

____ 30. ranching

c. Farming in fixed and permanent fields.

____ 31. sedentary cultivation

d. The commercial raising of herd livestock on a large landholding.

____ 32. subsistence agriculture

e. A system of monoculture for producing export crops requiring relatively large amounts of land and capital; originally dependent on slave labor.

Set 7

____ 33. suitcase farm

a. A type of agriculture characterized by land rotation in which temporary clearings are used for several years and then abandoned to be replaced by new clearings; also known as "slash-and-burn agriculture."

____ 34. survey pattern

b. The raising of food, including fruit, vegetables, meat, and milk, inside cities; especially common in the Third World.

____ 35. sustainability

c. In American commercial grain agriculture, a farm on which no one lives; planting and harvesting is done by hired migratory crews.

____ 36. swidden cultivation

d. A pattern of original land survey in an area.

____ 37. urban agriculture

e. The survival of a land-use system for centuries or millennia without destruction of the environmental base, allowing generation after generation to continue to live there.

REVIEW: Self-evaluation Tests

PART ONE: Multiple-choice

Circle the best answer for each question. When you are finished, read each question again with your selected answer. After you are satisfied with your practice test, use the Answer Key in the back of the Study Guide to check your responses.

1. About _____ percent of the world's working population is employed in agriculture.
   a. 2   b. 5   c. 15   d. 30   e. 40

2. In the United States the number of people involved in farming is less than _____ percent.
   a. 3   b. 20   c. 10   d. 12   e. 15

3. The agricultural practice of shifting cultivation is essentially:
   a. "slash-and-burn" agriculture.
   b. land-rotation system.
   c. found in Russia and other former Communist states.
   d. subsistence agriculture.
   e. none of the above

4. The hallmark of paddy rice farming is:
   a. Irish stone fences.
   b. environmental deterioration.
   c. high protein productivity.
   d. terraced paddy fields.
   e. the water buffalo.

5. Planting and harvesting the same land two or three times a year is known as:
   a. intertillage.
   b. crop-rotation.
   c. double-cropping.
   d. biannual agriculture.
   e. none of the above

6. The "green revolution" involved the introduction of:
   a. sugar cane.
   b. chemical fertilizers.
   c. organic methods.
   d. traditional practices of sustainability.
   e. gene banks.

7. Traditional Mediterranean agriculture is based in part on the cultivation of primarily barley and:
   a. oats.
   b. millet.
   c. rye.
   d. wheat.
   e. rice.

8. Nomadic herding is normally practiced in what type of environment?
   a. fertile valley floor
   b. tropical rain forest
   c. mountains or desert
   d. coastal plains
   e. temperate forests

9. Plantation agriculture usually maximizes the production of _____ for Europeans and Americans.
   a. coffee and tea
   b. grains
   c. cattle and other livestock
   d. luxury crops
   e. fruits and vegetables

10. Crops that tend to grow best in tropical highland regions are:
    a. coffee and tea.
    b. grains.
    c. luxury crops.
    d. fruits and vegetables.
    e. none of the above

11. Market gardening is also referred to as:
    a. neo-plantation.
    b. greenhouse farming.
    c. truck farming.
    d. market plantation.
    e. organic farming.

12. One of the most highly developed areas of commercial livestock fattening is:
    a. Alpine Europe.
    b. the Mediterranean region.
    c. the northeastern United States.
    d. the Corn Belt.
    e. Mesoamerica.

13. Fattening livestock, especially cattle, is an efficient method of protein production.
    a. True
    b. False

14. The major wheat-producing countries (producing 35 percent of the world's wheat) are the United States, Russia, Canada, Argentina, Kazakhstan, and:
    a. Germany.
    b. Australia.
    c. India.
    d. Italy.
    e. Ukraine.

15. Dairy farms located near large urban areas usually produce:
    a. butter.
    b. cheese.
    c. yogurt.
    d. processed milk.
    e. none of the above

16. Australia, New Zealand, South Africa, and Argentina produce 70 percent of the world's export of:
    a. beef.
    b. wool.
    c. coffee and tea.
    d. pork.
    e. fruit crops.

17. Mad cow disease is an example involving the issue of:
    a. GM foods.
    b. food fears.
    c. agribusiness.
    d. feedlot disease.
    e. salmonella.

18. Perhaps the oldest primary region of agriculture is:
    a. Southeast Asia.
    b. northwestern India.
    c. the Fertile Crescent.
    d. Mesoamerica.
    e. northeastern China.

19. The diffusion of many plant crops from the Western Hemisphere was accomplished by colonial powers, such as the Dutch and Portuguese.
    a. True
    b. False

20. What was developed to preserve what remains of domesticated plant variety?
    a. hybrid seeds
    b. the green revolution
    c. gene banks
    d. agriculture exclusion zones
    e. wild flower and plant nature preserves

21. A possible result of overgrazing of grasslands is:
    a. deforestation.
    b. soil saturation.
    c. desertification.
    d. increased protein production.
    e. none of the above

22. The Sahel is a critical region that is located:
    a. in southern India.
    b. in the Middle East.
    c. just south of the Sahara Desert.
    d. in southern Africa.
    e. in the interior of Australia.

23. Above all, most farmers rely upon:
    a. climatic stability.
    b. soil stability.
    c. access to water.
    d. temperature variation.
    e. low labor costs.

24. In von Thünen's isolated state model, the intensity of cultivation for any given crop increases as distance from the market increases.
    a. True
    b. False

PART TWO: Short-answer (probable essay-type questions)

25. Briefly summarize the modified version of von Thünen's isolated state model.

_____
_____
_____
_____

26. State the principle concepts and processes of aquaculture.

_____
_____
_____

27. Explain the difference between the American rectangular survey system and the "metes and bounds" survey system.

_____
_____
_____

28. What are the reasons for establishing "long-lot" farms *and* where are examples of these farms found?

_____
_____
_____

29. What are GM crops and where are they most common? Is this a problem for some?

_____
_____
_____

30. What are the important themes in Karl Zimmerer's research?

_____
_____
_____

31. Explain and describe the highly distinctive type of subsistence agriculture called paddy rice farming.

_____
_____
_____

32. State some of the problems as well as benefits associated with the green revolution.

_____
_____
_____

33. Briefly describe the problems of commercial livestock fattening in regard to nutritional efficiency.

_____
_____
_____

34. What is the difference between a "suitcase farm" and agribusiness?

_____
_____
_____

35. What are the major world regions of commercial dairying?

_____

_____

_____

36. Describe the conditions and setting in which agriculture first arose.

_____

_____

_____

37. What are some of the major crops domesticated by the native peoples of the Americas?

_____

_____

_____

38. Briefly discuss the theme of cultural adaptation in agricultural geography.

_____

_____

_____

39. Briefly explain the pros and cons of biofuels.

_____

_____

_____

40. What are some examples of food fears?

_____

_____

_____

41. What are some examples of indigenous technical knowledge?

_____

_____

_____

CHAPTER NINE

ECONOMIC GEOGRAPHY: INDUSTRIES, SERVICES, AND DEVELOPMENT

Extended Chapter Outline (including key terms)

I. What is Economic Development?
    A. Industrialization
    B. A model of economic development

II. Industrial and Service Regions
    A. Primary industries
    B. Secondary industries
    C. Services
        1. Transportation/communication services
        2. Producer services
        3. Consumer services, including tourism

III. Diffusion of Industry and Services
    A. Origins of the industrial revolution: cottage and guild industries
    B. Diffusion of the industrial revolution from Great Britain
    C. Locational shifts of secondary industry
        1. Transnational corporations
        2. Technopoles
        3. Deindustrialization

IV. Industrial-Economic Ecology
    A. Renewable resource crisis
    B. Acid rain
    C. Global climate change
        1. Global warming
        2. Greenhouse effect
    D. Ozone depletion
    E. Radioactive pollution
    F. Environmental sustainability
        1. Ecotourism
        2. Greens

V. Industrial-Economic Interaction
    A. Labor supply
        1. Labor-intensive industries
        2. Outsourcing
    B. Markets
    C. The political element; export processing zones
    D. Industrialization, globalization, and cultural change

V. Industrial-Economic Landscapes
   A. Industrial landscapes
   B. Other landscapes

LEARNING OBJECTIVES

After reading this chapter *and* studying the maps and illustrations, you should be able to:

1. Explain and define different categories of industry, including primary, secondary, and services.

2. Trace the locations, origin, and diffusion of the industrial revolution.

3. Understand the strong effects of industrialization upon Earth's habitat and its people.

4. Explain the difference between ozone depletion, greenhouse effect, and radioactive pollution as well as the consequences of each.

5. Discuss the causal factors in the shifting locations of economic activity.

6. Identify elements of various industrial landscapes and their origins.

7. Contemplate the massive impact (evident today) of the industrial revolution on Earth, its people, its resources, and its cultures.

SELECTED MAP READING AND INTERPRETATION

This section of the Study Guide is intended to heighten your map reading and interpretation skills. It will also help you apply the text readings to visual and spatial display of concepts, themes, and examples in human and cultural geography.

A world atlas (in print or online) will be very useful in completing this section of the Study Guide and will enhance your comprehension of the maps in the textbook. Ask your instructor to recommend an appropriate web site or atlas to purchase (or visit the map collection at your library). A world atlas is essential for your personal reference library, not only during this course, but throughout your college career.

After reading the text and then studying the accompanying map and its captions, answer the following questions.

FIGURE 9.1. World map of gross domestic product

1. Look at Europe. What do you think accounts for the east-west pattern of dollars per capita?

   _____

   _____

   _____

2. Does Africa show a north-south pattern of dollars per capita? Why or why not? What do you think are reasons for these locational patterns?

   _____

   _____

   _____

3. Why do you think that "no data" exists for the countries of North Korea, Western Sahara, Somalia, Iraq, and Montenegro? Explain.

   _____

   _____

   _____

FIGURE 9.3. Major regions of industry in Anglo-America

1. How would you delineate the major manufacturing belt in the United States and Canada?

   _____

   _____

   _____

2. Other than the major belt, what states share some of the minor regions? Why these locations, such as Portland-Seattle?

_____

_____

_____

FIGURE 9.8. Industrial regions and deindustrialization in Europe

1. If western Europe is the wealthiest part of Europe, why has so much industrial decline taken place there?

_____

_____

_____

2. What explains the situation that few luxury goods are manufactured east of Germany and Italy? Is this changing?

_____

_____

_____

3. Compare this map to a map showing the countries of the European Union. Do you see a relationship of any kind? Why or why not?

_____

_____

_____

4. Explain the shifting locations of various industries in Europe.

_____

_____

_____

FIGURE 9.9. Global sites of export processing zones

1. Explain the concentration of processing zones along the U.S.–Mexico border and also in Central America.

_____

_____

_____

2. What other major concentrations of export processing zones do you see and what do you think explains this pattern?

_____

_____

_____

FIGURE 9.12. Tropical rain forest of the Amazon Basin

1. About 10,000 square miles of this rain forest are cleared each year. What are the reasons for this massive activity?

   _____

   _____

   _____

2. Can you identify any patterns on this map in regard to terrain or rivers? You will also require a physical terrain map to answer this.

   _____

   _____

   _____

FIGURE 9.13. Comparison of the distribution of acid rain in the United States, 2001–2006

1. Which states suffer the worst deposition problems? Why?

   _____

   _____

   _____

2. Why do you think there are problems of acid precipitation in the Pacific Northwest?

   _____

   _____

   _____

3. What is the ecology of these patterns? Include climate, weather, and topography in your answer.

   _____

   _____

   _____

4. Compare this map to the map of the American industrial zones and manufacturing belt in this chapter. How does it compare?

   _____

   _____

   _____

FIGURE 9.16. Environmental Sustainability Index

1. Other than China, what countries rank lowest (worst) on this index?

   _____

   _____

   _____

2. What countries, such as Uruguay and Iceland, rank in the highest (best) category here?

_____

_____

_____

3. What global patterns does this map show? What can you interpret from them?

_____

_____

_____

MATCHING EXERCISES

Match each key term from the text to its definition. Answers are found at the end of this Study Guide.

Set 1

_____ 1. acid rain

a. Rainfall with much higher acidity than normal, caused by sulfur and nitrogen oxides derived from the burning of fossil fuels being flushed from the atmosphere by precipitation, with lethal effects for many plants and animals.

_____ 2. consumer services

b. The range of economic activities that facilitate the consumption of goods.

_____ 3. cottage industry

c. A traditional type of manufacturing in the pre–industrial revolution era, practiced on a small scale in individual rural households as a part-time occupation and designed to produce handmade goods for local consumption.

_____ 4. deindustrialization

d. The process by which an agricultural society moves toward industrialization and (usually) higher patterns of income.

_____ 5. economic development

e. The decline of primary and secondary industry, accompanied by a rise in the service sectors of the industrial economy.

Set 2

_____ 6. ecotourism

a. Designated areas of countries where governments create conditions conducive to export-oriented production.

_____ 7. export processing zones (EPZs)

b. An area along a limited-access highway that houses offices and other services associated with high-tech industries.

_____ 8. global warming

c. A process in which the increased release of carbon dioxide and other gases into the atmosphere, caused by industrial activity and deforestation, permits solar short-wave heat radiation to reach the Earth's surface but blocks long-wave outgoing radiation, causing a thermal imbalance and global heating.

_____ 9. greenhouse effect

d. Responsible travel that does not harm ecosystems or the well-being of local people.

_____ 10. Greens

e. Activists and organizations, including political parties, whose central concern is addressing environmental deterioration.

_____ 11. guild industry

f. The pronounced climatic warming of the Earth that has occurred since about 1920 and particularly since the 1970s.

_____ 12. high-tech corridor

g. A traditional type of manufacturing in the pre–industrial revolution era, involving handmade goods of high quality manufactured by highly skilled artisans who resided in towns and cities.

Set 3

_____ 13. industrial revolution

_____ 14. industrialization

_____ 15. labor-intensive industry

_____ 16. *maquiladora*

_____ 17. market

a. The transformation of raw materials into commodities, or the process by which a society moves from subsistence agriculture toward mass production based on machinery and industry.

b. An industry for which labor costs represent a large proportion of total production costs.

c. The geographical area in which a product may be sold in a volume and at a price profitable to the manufacturer.

d. A U.S.-owned assembly planted located on the Mexican side of the U.S.-Mexico border.

e. A series of inventions and innovations, arising in England in the 1700s, that led to the use of machines and inanimate power in the manufacturing process.

Set 4

_____ 18. outsource

_____ 19. postindustrial phase

_____ 20. primary industry

_____ 21. producer services

_____ 22. renewable resource

a. The physical separation of some economic activities from the main production facility, usually for the purpose of employing cheaper labor.

b. An industry engaged in the extraction of natural resources, such as agriculture, lumbering, and mining.

c. A resource that is not depleted if wisely used, such as forests, water, fishing grounds, and agricultural land.

d. A society characterized by the dominance of the service sectors of economic activity.

e. The range of economic activities required by producers of goods.

Set 5

_____ 23. secondary industry

_____ 24. services

_____ 25. sustainability

_____ 26. technopole

_____ 27. transnational corporations

_____ 28. transportation/ communication services

a. The range of economic activities that provide services to industry.

b. The survival of a land-use system for centuries or millennia without destruction of the environmental base, allowing generation after generation to continue to live there.

c. A center of high-tech manufacturing and information-based industry.

d. An industry engaged in processing raw materials into finished products; manufacturing.

e. Companies that have international production, marketing, and management facilities.

f. The range of economic activities that provide transport and communication to businesses.

REVIEW: Self-evaluation Tests

PART ONE: Multiple-choice

Circle the best answer for each question. When you are finished, read each question again with your selected answer. After you are satisfied with your practice test, use the Answer Key in the back of the Study Guide to check your responses.

1. The processing of raw materials into a more usable form is:
   a. primary industry.
   b. secondary industry.
   c. service industry.
   d. consumer industry.
   e. producer industry.

2. Agriculture is considered to be a:
   a. primary industry.
   b. secondary industry.
   c. service industry.
   d. consumer industry.
   e. producer industry.

3. The extraction of nonrenewable resources is a:
   a. primary industry.
   b. secondary industry.
   c. service industry.
   d. consumer industry.
   e. producer industry.

4. Legal services, retailing, and advertising are all considered:
   a. primary industry.
   b. secondary industry.
   c. service industry.
   d. extraction industry.
   e. manufacturing industry.

5. Consumer-related services, such as education, are considered:
   a. primary industry.
   b. secondary industry.
   c. service industry.
   d. extraction industry.
   e. manufacturing industry.

6. The American manufacturing melt is located:
   a. from Los Angeles to New York City.
   b. primarily in the Lower South.

    c. from Chicago to Pittsburgh.
    d. around the Great Lakes and Northeast states.
    e. in New England and the Piedmont.

7. Multinational or transnational companies are also referred to as:
    a. global corporations.
    b. international enterprises.
    c. inter-regional industries.
    d. global conglomerates.
    e. none of the above

8. In Russia and the Ukraine the most important mode of industrial transport is:
    a. highways.
    b. railways.
    c. airways.
    d. waterways.
    e. none of the above

9. While the cottage and guild industry systems were similar in many respects, only cottage industry depended on hand labor.
    a. True
    b. False

10. The initial breakthrough in the industrial revolution occurred in:
    a. the German steel industry.
    b. the British smelting processes.
    c. Dutch papermaking.
    d. the British steel industry.
    e. British textiles.

11. The industrial revolution diffused from its place of origin first to:
    a. British colonies in North America.
    b. British colonies in Africa and India.
    c. continental Europe.
    d. France.
    e. the West Midlands of England.

12. The worst area of acid rain pollution in the United States is:
    a. greater Los Angeles.
    b. the Great Lakes states.
    c. Texas and Louisiana.
    d. the Great Plains.
    e. none of the above

13. The basic cause of acid rain is the burning of:
    a. wood.
    b. coal.
    c. oil.
    d. fossil fuels.
    e. high sulfur coal.

14. Over 90 lakes are "dead" from acid rain in this seemingly pristine mountain range.
    a. Adirondacks
    b. Smoky Mountains
    c. Catskills
    d. Rockies
    e. Canadian Rockies

15. Greenhouse effect is caused primarily by:
    a. burning coal.
    b. burning fossil fuels.
    c. ozone depletion.
    d. the hole in the ozone layer.
    e. none of the above

16. Carbon dioxide gases permit solar short-wave radiation to reach the Earth's surface and allow outgoing long-wave radiation to escape.
    a. True
    b. False

17. Ozone layer depletion is caused by:
    a. fossil fuels.
    b. greenhouse effect.
    c. global warming.
    d. manufactured chemicals.
    e. radioactive waste .

18. A hotspot of ecotourism is:
    a. Uganda.
    b. the Rocky Mountains.
    c. the Great Lakes.
    d. the Sahara Desert.
    e. the Arctic.

19. In nearly all industrial site locations, a major factor is:
    a. water supply.
    b. politics.
    c. labor supply.
    d. electricity supply.
    e. climate.

20. Coastal, often scenic, fishing villages from Norway to Portugal are part of the industrial landscape.
    a. True
    b. False

PART TWO: Short-answer (probable essay-type questions)

21. What and where is the origin of the industrial revolution?

_____
_____
_____

22. What was the spatial and temporal pattern of industrial mobility and diffusion?

_____
_____
_____

23. What are primary industrial activities?

_____
_____
_____

24. What is the difference between primary and secondary industrial activities?

_____
_____
_____

25. Where is most secondary industrial activity located in North America?

_____
_____
_____

26. What was the diffusion pattern of the industrial revolution in Europe?

_____
_____
_____

27. Why did the highway displace the railroad in America as a major factor in regard to industry?

_____
_____
_____

28. What are the sources of radioactive pollution?

_____

_____

_____

29. How is acid rain created and what regions does it strongly affect?

_____

_____

_____

30. What are the major problems associated with dependency on fossil fuels?

_____

_____

_____

31. What are the main differences between greenhouse effect, ozone depletion, and global warming?

_____

_____

_____

32. Explain the causal factors of greenhouse effect.

_____

_____

_____

33. Describe some environmental factors in industrial location.

_____

_____

_____

34. Describe the various relationships between labor and industrial location.

_____

_____

_____

35. What all-encompassing cultural changes were brought about by the industrial revolution?

_____

_____

_____

36. Explain the various impacts politics can have on industry.

_____

_____

_____

37. Describe industrial landscape from the categories of primary, secondary, and service industries.

_____

_____

_____

38. Provide examples of how the industrial landscape is interpreted by some humanists.

_____

_____

_____

39. How does international tourism impact economics and cultures globally and locally?

_____

_____

_____

40. What is ecotourism and where is it usually practiced? By whom?

_____

_____

_____

CHAPTER TEN

URBANIZATION

Extended Chapter Outline (including key terms)

I. Urban Culture Regions
    A. Patterns and processes of urbanization
    B. Impacts of urbanization
        1. Megacities
        2. Primate cities

II. Origin and Diffusion of the City
    A. Models for the rise of cities
        1. Technical factors: hydraulic civilization model
        2. Religious factors
        3. Political factors
        4. Multiple factors
    B. Urban hearth areas
        1. Cosmomagical cities and axis mundi
    C. Diffusion of the city from hearth areas
    D. Rural to urban migration
    E. The globalization of cities
        1. Global cities
        2. Globalizing cities

III. The Ecology of Urban Location
    A. Site and situation
    B. Defensive sites
    C. Trade-route sites
    D. Natural disasters

IV. Cultural Interaction in Urban Geography
    A. Central-place theory
        1. Threshold
        2. Range
        3. Hinterland

V. Urban Cultural Landscapes
    A. Globalizing cities in the developing world
        1. Squatter settlements, barriadas
    B. Apartheid and postapartheid city
    C. Socialist and postsocialist city

LEARNING OBJECTIVES

After reading this chapter *and* studying the maps and illustrations, you should be able to:

1. Discuss possible definitions of the "city" and the meaning of urbanized population.

2. Explain various theories dealing with the origin and diffusion of the city.

3. Demonstrate knowledge of urban hearth areas and the ten largest urban centers today.

4. Discuss the evolution of urban landscapes.

5. Understand the problems of the globalized city.

6. Explain the causal factors that led to the capitalist city.

7. Discuss the impact of industrialization on city structure.

8. Understand various models of cities in developing countries.

9. Describe the post-apartheid and postsocialist cities.

10. Interpret with new understanding various cities with which you are familiar.

SELECTED MAP READING AND INTERPRETATION

This section of the Study Guide is intended to heighten your map reading and interpretation skills. It will also help you apply the text readings to visual and spatial display of concepts, themes, and examples in human and cultural geography.

A world atlas (in print or online) will be very useful in completing this section of the Study Guide and will enhance your comprehension of the maps in the textbook. Ask your instructor to recommend an appropriate web site or atlas to purchase (or visit the map collection at your library). A world atlas is essential for your personal reference library, not only during this course, but throughout your college career.

After reading the text and then studying the accompanying map and its captions, answer the following questions.

FIGURE 10.1. Urbanized population in the world

1. Although China and India have more people than any other countries, what accounts for the relatively low amount of urbanization?

   _____

   _____

   _____

2. Can you think of environmental factors for the high percentage of urbanization in such countries as Australia, Saudi Arabia, and Libya? What do these countries have in common?

   _____

   _____

   _____

3. Speculate the reasons behind the apparent difference between the Eastern and Western Hemispheres in term of urbanized population.

   _____

   _____

   _____

FIGURE 10.3. The world's first cities arose in six urban hearth areas

1. In which countries are these ancient hearth areas, such as Mesopotamia, located today?

   _____

   _____

   _____

2. What are the rivers associated, if any, with each of these specific hearth areas?

_____

_____

_____

FIGURE 10.14. Large cities in relation to current climate-related hazards

1. Where are the highest risk cities located in North America?

_____

_____

_____

2. Is there a correlation shown between high risk hazard areas and urbanization? Why or why not?

_____

_____

_____

3. What global patterns can you identify here? Do you see a pattern of physical environments or terrain related to hazard areas?

_____

_____

_____

MATCHING EXERCISES

Match each key term from the text to its definition. Answers are found at the end of this Study Guide.

Set 1

_____ 1. agricultural surplus

_____ 2. apartheid

_____ 3. axis mundi

_____ 4. barriada

_____ 5. central place

a. A town or city engaged primarily in the service stages of production; a regional center.

b. The amount of food grown by a society that exceeds the demands of its population.

c. The symbolic center of cosmomagical cities, often demarcated by a large, vertical structure.

d. An illegal housing settlement, usually made up of temporary shelters, that surround large cities; often referred to as a *squatter settlement.*

e. In South Africa, a policy of racial segregation and discrimination against non-European groups.

Set 2

_____ 6. central-place theory

_____ 7. cosmomagical city

_____ 8. defensive site

_____ 9. global city

_____ 10. globalizing city

_____ 11. hinterland

_____ 12. hydraulic civilization

_____ 13. megacity

a. A type of city that is laid out in accordance with religious principles, characteristic of very early cities, particularly in China.

b. A location from which a city can be easily defended.

c. A city being shaped by the new global economy and culture.

d. The area surrounding a city and influenced by it.

e. A term that refers to a particularly large urban center.

f. A set of models designed to explain the spatial distribution of urban service centers.

g. A city that is a control center of the global economy.

h. A civilization based on large-scale irrigation.

Set 3

_____ 14. primate city

_____ 15. range

_____ 16. site

_____ 17. situation

a. A city of large size and dominant power within a country.

b. The regional setting of a city.

c. In central-place theory, the average maximum distance people will travel to purchase a good or service.

d. The local setting of a city.

Set 4

____	18. squatter settlement		a. An illegal housing settlement, usually made up of temporary shelters, that surrounds a large city.
____	19. threshold		b. In central-place theory, the size of the population required to make provision of goods and services economically feasible.
____	20. trade-route site		c. A place for a city at a significant point on a transportation route.
____	21. urban hearth area		d. The proportion of a country's population living in cities.
____	22. urbanized population		e. A region in which the world's first cities evolved.

REVIEW: Self-evaluation Tests

PART ONE: Multiple-choice

Circle the best answer for each question. When you are finished, read each question again with your selected answer. After you are satisfied with your practice test, use the Answer Key in the back of the Study Guide to check your responses.

1. Urbanized population refers to a country's:
   a. number of cities.
   b. number of cities over 100,000 in population.
   c. percentage of urban population.
   d. ratio of urban to rural population.
   e. none of the above

2. The U.S. Census Bureau defines a city as a densely populated area of _____ people or more.
   a. 2500
   b. 5000
   c. 10,000
   d. 20,000
   e. 50,000

3. The term "global cities" refers to cities having populations of at least:
   a. 500,000.
   b. 1,000,000.
   c. 5,000,000.
   d. 10,000,000.
   e. none of the above

4. Which of the following cities is NOT ranked in the world's ten largest metropolitan areas?
   a. Seoul
   b. Delhi
   c. Moscow
   d. New York
   e. Mumbai

5. The city that dominates the political, economic, and cultural life of a country is the _____ city.
   a. capital
   b. most populous
   c. vanguard
   d. primate
   e. growth pole

6. The origin of cities is strongly related to:
   a. plant and animal domestication.
   b. improved transportation networks.
   c. warfare and defense.
   d. improved building techniques.
   e. all of the above

7. The hydraulic civilization model can be tied to all of the following urban hearths *except*:
   a. China.
   b. Mesoamerica.
   c. Egypt.
   d. Mesopotamia (Iraq).
   e. Indus River valley.

8. Cosmomagical cities exhibit the three spatial characteristics of a _____, symbolic center, and cardinal direction orientation.
   a. walled circumference
   b. walled outer city
   c. universe-like form
   d. wheel spoke form
   e. moat or bulwark

9. The pattern of functional land use within a city is referred to as:
   a. urban morphology.
   b. functional development.
   c. functional zonation.
   d. spatial landscapes.
   e. urban land use.

10. The place for public use and markets in ancient Greek cities was the:
    a. agora.
    b. citadel.
    c. forum.
    d. acropolis.
    e. castra.

11. Globalizing cities strongly involves:
    a. migration.
    b. postindustrialism.
    c. geopolitics.
    d. religion, especially Islam.
    e. the automotive industry.

12. The regional setting of an urban location is called the:
    a. site.
    b. node.
    c. ecological niche.
    d. situation.
    e. none of the above

13. Mexico City, Montreal, New York City, and Venice are all examples of:
    a. limited access cities.
    b. colonial cities.
    c. river-island sites.
    d. acropolis sites.
    e. defensive sites.

14. Critical to central-place theory is the fact that different goods and services vary both
    in _____ and range.
    a. spatial distribution
    b. quality
    c. quantity
    d. threshold
    e. access

15. Large-scale squatter settlements are a typical feature of many:
    a. Mexican cities.
    b. European and Russian cities.
    c. "developing" world cities.
    d. former French and Portuguese colonies.
    e. North African and Middle East cities.

PART TWO: Short-answer (probable essay-type questions)

16. Briefly explain "threshold" and "range" in central-place theory.

    _____
    _____
    _____

17. What did Christaller add to central-place theory in his second model?

    _____
    _____
    _____

18. Describe a squatter settlement, including a couple of actual examples.

    _____
    _____
    _____

19. Clearly explain the difference between city site and situation.

_____
_____
_____

20. What are characteristics of the postsocialist city?

_____
_____
_____

21. What is meant by "capitalist city"?

_____
_____
_____

22. Describe some main features of the institution of kingship.

_____
_____
_____

23. What are the spatial features associated with cosmomagical cities?

_____
_____
_____

24. Discuss an argument concerning the diffusion of the city from hearth areas.

_____
_____
_____

25. What are characteristics of the postapartheid city?

_____
_____
_____

CHAPTER ELEVEN

INSIDE THE CITY

Extended Chapter Outline (including key terms)

I. Urban Culture Regions
    A. Downtowns, central business district (CBD)
    B. Residential areas and neighborhoods
       1. Social culture region
       2. Ethnic culture region
       3. Census tracts
    C. Homelessness

II. Cultural Diffusion in the City
    A. Centralization: economic and social advantages
    B. Suburbanization and decentralization
       1. Uneven development
       2. Socioeconomic factors, lateral commuting
       3. Public policy, restrictive covenants, and redlining
       4. The costs of decentralization; checkerboarding and in-filling
    C. Gentrification
       1. Economic and political factors
       2. Sexuality and gentrification
       3. Costs of gentrification
    D. Immigration and new ethnic neighborhoods

III. The Cultural Ecology of the City
    A. Urban weather and climate; heat islands and dust domes
    B. Urban hydrology
    C. Urban vegetation

IV. Cultural Interaction and Models of the City
    A. Concentric zone model
    B. Sector model
    C. Multiple-nuclei model

V. Urban Landscapes
    A. Themes in cityscape study (urban morphology, functional zonation)
    B. Megalopolis and edge cities
    C. New urban and suburban landscapes
       1. Shopping malls
       2. Office parks and high-tech corridors
       3. Master-planned communities
       4. Festival settings
       5. Militarized space
       6. Decline of public space

LEARNING OBJECTIVES

After reading this chapter *and* studying the maps and illustrations, you should be able to:

1. Identify and describe various and distinct urban culture regions.

2. Understand the concept, views, perception, and importance of the "neighborhood" and its role in everyday life.

3. Explain the difference between and the pros and cons of centralization and decentralization of the city.

4. Understand the elements of the urban ecosystem and its impact on society.

5. Identify various city models and relate them to actual cities.

6. Understand the elements of the city landscape and its causal factors.

7. Identify symbolic, cultural, and perceptive elements of the city environment.

8. Understand the role of globalization and the dynamics of city life.

9. Begin to look at and interpret, with new awareness, the cities and neighborhoods around you.

SELECTED MAP READING AND INTERPRETATION

This section of the Study Guide is intended to heighten your map reading and interpretation skills. It will also help you apply the text readings to visual and spatial display of concepts, themes, and examples in human and cultural geography.

A world atlas (in print or online) will be very useful in completing this section of the Study Guide and will enhance your comprehension of the maps in the textbook. Ask your instructor to recommend an appropriate web site or atlas to purchase (or visit the map collection at your library). A world atlas is essential for your personal reference library, not only during this course, but throughout your college career.

After reading the text and then studying the accompanying map and its captions, answer the following questions.

FIGURE 11.11. Map indicating the location of 10 metropolitan areas . . .

1. Why is immigration focused on these specific cities?

    _____
    _____
    _____
    _____

2. Why do you think that some major cities, such as Detroit, Seattle, Denver, Cleveland, and Phoenix, are not included in these statistics?

    _____
    _____
    _____

MATCHING EXERCISES

Match each key term from the text to its definition. Answers are found at the end of this Study Guide.

Set 1

_____ 1. agglomeration

a. Diffusion forces that encourage people or businesses to locate in the central city.

_____ 2. census tracts

b. The central portion of a city, characterized by high-density land uses.

_____ 3. central business district (CBD)

c. Small districts used by the U.S. Census Bureau to survey the population.

_____ 4. centralizing forces

d. A snowballing geographical process by which secondary and service industrial activities become clustered in cities and compact industrial regions in order to share infrastructure and markets.

Set 2

_____ 5. checkerboard development

a. An urban landscape.

_____ 6. cityscape

b. A social model that depicts a city as five areas bounded by concentric rings.

_____ 7. concentric-zone model

c. The decline of primary and secondary industry, accompanied by a rise in the service sectors of the industrial economy.

_____ 8. decentralizing forces

d. Diffusion forces that encourage people or businesses to locate outside the central city.

_____ 9. deindustrialization

e. A mixture of farmlands and housing tracts.

Set 3

_____ 10. dust dome

a. A pollution layer over a city that is thickest at the center of the city.

_____ 11. edge city

b. The displacement of lower-income residents by higher-income residents as buildings in deteriorated areas of city centers are restored.

_____ 12. ethnic culture region

c. A new urban cluster of economic activity that surrounds nineteenth-century downtowns.

_____ 13. festival setting

d. A multiuse redevelopment project that is built around a particular setting, often one with a historical association.

_____ 14. functional zonation

e. An area occupied by people of similar ethnic background who share traits of ethnicity, such as language and migration history.

_____ 15. gentrification

f. The pattern of land uses within a city; the existence of areas with differing functions, such as residential, commercial, and governmental.

Set 4

_____ 16. heat island

a. A city that is easy to decipher, with clear pathways, edges, nodes, districts, and landmarks.

_____ 17. high-tech corridor

b. An area of warmer temperatures at the center of a city, caused by the urban concentration of heat-retaining concrete, brick, and asphalt.

_____ 18. homelessness

c. Traveling from one suburb to another in going from home to work.

_____ 19. in-filling

d. An area along a limited-access highway that houses offices and other services associated with high-tech industries.

_____ 20. lateral commuting

e. A temporary or permanent condition of not having a legal home address.

_____ 21. legible city

f. New building on empty parcels of land within a checkerboard pattern of development.

Set 5

_____ 22. master-planned communities

a. A large urban region formed as several urban areas spread and merge, such as Boswash, the region including Boston, New York, and Washington, D.C.

_____ 23. megalopolis

b. A model that depicts a city growing from several separate focal points.

_____ 24. multiple-nuclei model

c. Large-scale residential developments that include, in addition to architecturally compatible housing units, planned recreational facilities, schools, and security measures.

_____ 25. neighborhood

d. A small social area within a city where residents share values and concerns and interact with one another on a daily basis.

_____ 26. office park

e. A term used to describe cultural landscapes with various layers and historical "messages." Geographers use this term to reinforce the notion of the landscape as a text that can be read.

_____ 27. palimpsest

f. A cluster of office buildings, usually located along an interstate, often forming the nucleus of an edge city.

Set 6

_____ 28. redlining

a. The form and structure of cities, including street patterns and the size and shape of buildings.

_____ 29. restrictive covenant

b. An area in a city where many of the residents share social traits such as income, education, and stage of life.

_____ 30. sector model

c. A practice by banks and mortgage companies of demarcating areas considered to be high risk for housing loans.

_____ 31. social culture region

d. A statement written into a property deed that restricts the use of the land in some way; often used to prohibit certain groups of people from buying property.

_____ 32. uneven development

e. An economic model that depicts a city as a series of pie-shaped wedges.

_____ 33. urban morphology

f. The tendency for industry to develop in a core-periphery pattern, enriching the industrialized countries of the core and impoverishing the less industrialized periphery. This term is also used to describe urban patterns in which suburban areas are enriched while the inner city is impoverished.

REVIEW: Self-evaluation Tests

PART ONE: Multiple-choice

Circle the best answer for each question. When you are finished, read each question again with your selected answer. After you are satisfied with your practice test, use the Answer Key in the back of the Study Guide to check your responses.

1. An excellent method of defining social regions is to isolate one social trait and plot its distribution within a city by using:
   a. aerial maps.
   b. satellite imagery.
   c. census tracts.
   d. telephone directories.
   e. property tax records.

2. The neighborhood concept is critical to cultural geography because it:
   a. recognizes the sentiment people have for places.
   b. provides examples of race relations within cities.
   c. illustrates and explores urban ecology.
   d. helps us understand spatial structures of cities.
   e. none of the above

3. An important economic advantage to central city location has traditionally been:
   a. product cost.
   b. advertising.
   c. close proximity to major transport networks.
   d. accessibility.
   e. all of the above

4. Agglomeration or clustering is considered:
   a. an economic disadvantage.
   b. an economic advantage.
   c. the hope for the future of neighborhoods.
   d. an out-of date-method of urban planning.
   e. a hallmark of North American cities, but not European cities

5. Today, many people travel to work from suburb to suburb. This is termed:
   a. suburban dependency.
   b. "by-pass commuting."
   c. lateral commuting.
   d. "highway by-pass" commuting.
   e. none of the above

6. The government body known as the FHA is an abbreviation for:
   a. Fair Housing Act.
   b. Federal Home Association.
   c. Family Housing Act.
   d. Federal Housing Act.
   e. Federal Housing Administration.

7. A practice in which banks and mortgage companies designate areas considered to be at high risk for loans is:
   a. redistricting.
   b. redlining.
   c. covenants.
   d. blacklisting.
   e. none of the above

8. The movement of middle-class people into deteriorated areas of the city center is referred to as:
   a. urban revitalization.
   b. urban renewal.
   c. gentrification.
   d. insanity.
   e. reverse out-migration.

9. Lower-income people of the inner city are often displaced by the process of:
   a. urban sprawl.
   b. urban housing projects.
   c. gentrification.
   d. homelessness.
   e. reverse out-migration.

10. The study of the relationship between an organism and its physical environment is called:
    a. physical geography.
    b. physical geology.
    c. Earth Science.
    d. ecology.
    e. cultural ecology.

11. The direction of city growth, the patterning of social regions, and the routing of transportation can all be influenced by:
    a. topography.
    b. river and waterway patterns.
    c. climate.
    d. seasonality.
    e. temperature variation.

12. The heat generation of a city produces a large mass of warmer air sitting over the city called the urban heat island.
    a. True
    b. False

13. During the summer, a city center is warmer than its suburbs.
    a. True
    b. False

14. The concentric zone model of Burgess has five zones. Zone 2, characterized by a mixed pattern of industrial and residential land use, is considered a _____ zone.
    a. stable
    b. blue-collar
    c. transitional
    d. better housing
    e. gentrified

15. The area of the concentric zone model characterized by commuters and high-income families is zone _____ .
    a. 1
    b. 2
    c. 3
    d. 4
    e. 5

16. The sector model of urban land-use was developed by:
    a. Burgess.
    b. Hoyt.
    c. Harris.
    d. Ullman.
    e. none of the above

17. The model that maintains that a city develops with equal intensity around various points is the _____ model.
    a. sector
    b. concentric zone
    c. urban growth
    d. multiple nuclei
    e. none of the above

18. A palimpsest is a:
    a. section of most American cities.
    b. section of most European cities.
    c. critical part of the sector model.
    d. reference to transport planning.
    e. parchment used over and over for written messages.

19. A cemetery may be considered part of a city's:
    a. park system.
    b. symbolic landscape.
    c. palimpsest.
    d. CBD.
    e. all of the above

20. Which of the following is considered a landmark?
    a. city hall
    b. railway depot
    c. industrial smokestack
    d. White Castle restaurant
    e. all of the above

21. Shopping malls in North America are _____ spaces.
    a. eternal
    b. urban
    c. private
    d. open
    e. public

22. Many U.S. cities have a pattern of leap-frog expansion, and then in-filling, to use all of the space inside the city limits.
    a. True
    b. False

PART TWO: Short-answer (probable essay-type questions)

23. What human factors define a neighborhood?

    _____
    _____
    _____

24. What is meant by the "city as palimpsest"?

    _____
    _____
    _____

25. Describe elements of a neighborhood that you are familiar with.

_____

_____

_____

26. What are the elements of Homer Hoyt's urban model?

_____

_____

_____

27. List some symbols and landmarks of the urban environment.

_____

_____

_____

28. How do cities affect the natural environment and ecology?

_____

_____

_____

29. What are some criticisms of the concentric zone model?

_____

_____

_____

30. Briefly discuss the role of race and gender in the urban mosaic.

_____

_____

_____

31. Describe the concept of the shopping mall as a social center.

_____

_____

_____

32. What are some of the costs of city decentralization?

_____

_____

_____

33. Are neighborhoods found in the suburbs? Why or why not?

_____

_____

_____

34. What are some of the human costs of gentrification?

_____
_____
_____

35. How does topography influence city growth and structure?

_____
_____
_____

36. Is urban hydrology a factor in the future of cities? How and why?

_____
_____
_____

37. What are the problems of defining "homelessness"?

_____
_____
_____

38. Describe the composition of the new ethnic neighborhoods.

_____
_____
_____

39. What are some patterns of new ethnic migration and city destinations in North America?

_____
_____
_____

ANSWER KEY

CHAPTER 1

Matching Questions
1. b, 2. e, 3. a, 4. f, 5. d, 6. c, 7. a, 8.e, 9. b, 10. c, 11. d, 12. f, 13. c, 14. a, 15. b, 16. e, 17. f, 18. d, 19. b, 20, d, 21. f, 22, e, 23. c, 24. a, 25. d, 26. b, 27. a, 28. c, 29. e, 30. f, 31. c, 32. f, 33. e, 34. d, 35. b, 36. a, 37. d, 38. a, 39. f, 40. e, 41. b, 42. c, 43. b, 44. a, 45. c

Self-Evaluation Test
1.c 2.b 3.d 4.c 5.b 6.b 7.b 8.b 9.d 10.e
11.c 12.a 13.a 14.c 15.c 16.b 17.c 18.a 19.d 20.b
21.e 22.a 23.c

CHAPTER 2

Matching Questions
1. b, 2. a, 3. d, 4. c, 5. f, 6. e, 7. d, 8. e, 9. f, 10. a, 11. c, 12. b, 13. d, 14. a, 15. c, 16. b

Self-Evaluation Test
1.c 2.a 3.d 4.b 5.e 6.b 7.c 8.a
9.e 10.c 11.e 12.b 13.b 14.d 15.c
16.a 17.e 18.a 19.a 20.e 21.d 22.c
23.d 24.a 25.b 26.d 27.d 28.a 29.c

CHAPTER 3

Matching Questions
1. c, 2. a, 3. b, 4. f, 5. e, 6. d, 7. d, 8. f, 9. c, 10. b, 11. e, 12. a, 13. c, 14. a, 15. d, 16. b, 17. f, 18. g, 19. e, 20. a, 21. c, 22. b

Self-Evaluation Test
1.e 2.c 3.b 4.a 5.c 6.a 7.b 8.a 9.d 10.c
11.d 12.c or d 13.a 14.a 15.b 16.b 17.b
18.d 19.e 20.d 21.b 22.b 23.d

CHAPTER 4

Matching Questions
1. f, 2. b, 3. d, 4. e, 5. c, 6. a, 7. d, 8. a, 9. b, 10. e, 11.c, 12. a., 13. b, 14. d, 15. c

Self-Evaluation Test
1.d 2.e 3.c 4.b 5.a 6.d 7.d 8.b 9.a 10.a
11.e 12.b 13.c 14.c 15.d 16.c 17.d 18.a 19.d
20.d 21.b 22.a

CHAPTER 5

Matching Questions
1. f, 2. a, 3. b, 4. e, 5. c, 6. d, 7. b, 8. c, 9. e, 10. d, 11. a, 12. f, 13. b, 14. a, 15. d, 16. e, 17. c, 18. c, 19. d, 20. f, 21. e, 22. b, 23. a

Self-Evaluation Test
1.c 2.b 3.a 4.e 5.e 6.a 7.b 8.c 9.c 10.c
11.a 12.b 13.c 14.b 15.a 16.c 17.c 18.e 19.c
20.a 21.a 22.e

CHAPTER 6

Matching Questions
1. f, 2. e, 3. d, 4. c, 5. b, 6. a, 7. c, 8. a, 9. b, 10. f, 11. d, 12. e, 13. c, 14. b, 15. f, 16. a, 17. e, 18. d, 19. c, 20. a, 21. b, 22. f, 23. e, 24. d, 25. b, 26. a, 27. c, 28. e, 29. d, 30. a, 31. b, 32. c

Self-Evaluation Test
1.d 2.a 3.c 4.b 5.d 6.b 7.b 8.d 9.b 10.b
11.c 12.e 13.a 14.b 15.e 16.a 17.a 18.e 19.c
20.d 21.b 22.e 23.d 24.d

CHAPTER 7
Matching Questions
1. a, 2. c, 3. e, 4. f, 5. d, 6. b, 7. c, 8. a, 9. d, 10. e, 11. f, 12. b, 13. c, 14. d, 15. b, 16. a

Self-Evaluation Test
1.b 2.c 3.e 4.d 5.c 6.a 7.d 8.e 9.e 10.b
11.a 12.d 13.d 14.d 15.b 16.b 17.c 18.a
19.b 20.a 21.a 22.e

CHAPTER 8

Matching Questions
1. c, 2. e, 3. d, 4. b, 5. a, 6. a, 7. b, 8. e, 9. f, 10. g, 11. d, 12. c, 13. b, 14. a, 15. c, 16, d.
17. e, 18. c, 19. e, 20. d, 21. b, 22. a, 23. b, 24. a, 25. d, 26. e, 27. c, 28. b, 29. e, 30. d, 31.
c, 32. a, 33. c, 34. d, 35. e, 36. a, 37. b

Self-Evaluation Test
1.e 2.a 3.b 4.d 5.c 6.b 7.d 8.c 9.d
10.a 11.c 12.d 13.b 14.e 15.d 16.b 17.b 18.c
19.a 20.c 21.c 22.c 23.a 24.b

CHAPTER 9

Matching Questions
1. a, 2. b, 3. c, 4. e, 5. d, 6. d, 7. a, 8. f, 9. c, 10. e, 11. g, 12. b, 13. e, 14. a, 15. b, 16. d,
17. c, 18. a, 19. d, 20. b, 21. e, 22. c, 23. d, 24. a, 25. b, 26. c, 27. e, 28. f

Self-Evaluation Test
1.b 2.a 3.a 4.c 5.d 6.d 7.b 8.b 9.b 10.e
11.c 12.b 13.d 14.a 15.b 16.b 17.d 18.a
19.a 20.a

CHAPTER 10

Matching Questions
1. b, 2. e, 3. c, 4. d, 5. a, 6. f, 7. a, 8. b, 9. g, 10. d, 11. d, 12. h, 13. e, 14. a, 15. c, 16. d,
17. b, 18. a, 19. b, 20. c, 21. e, 22. d

Self-Evaluation Test
1.c 2.a 3.e 4 .c 5.d 6.a 7.b 8.c 9.c 10.a
11.a 12.d 13c 14.d 15.c

CHAPTER 11

Matching Questions
1. d, 2. c, 3. b, 4. a, 5. e, 6. a, 7. b, 8. d, 9. c, 10. a, 11. c, 12. e, 13. d, 14. f, 15. b, 16. b,
17. d, 18. e, 19. f, 20. c, 21. a, 22. c, 23. a, 24. b, 25. d, 26. f, 27. e, 28. c, 29. d, 30. e, 31.
b, 32. f, 33. a

Self-Evaluation Test

1.c 2.e 3.d 4.b 5.c 6.e 7.b 8.c 9.c 10.d
11.a 12.a 13.a 14.c 15.e 16.b 17.d
18.e 19. b 20.b 21.e 22.b